How to Think with Intention:

How to Identify, Transform, and Apply Mindsets for Control, Confidence, Growth, and Freedom

By Patrick King

Social Interaction and Conversation Coach at
www.PatrickKingConsulting.com

Table of Contents

HOW TO THINK WITH INTENTION: *HOW TO IDENTIFY, TRANSFORM, AND APPLY MINDSETS FOR CONTROL, CONFIDENCE, GROWTH, AND FREEDOM* — 3

TABLE OF CONTENTS — 5

CHAPTER 1: TURN OFF AUTOPILOT — 7
INTENTIONAL THINKING IN FOUR STEPS — 19

CHAPTER 2: THE BLOCK OF SELF-DOUBT — 29
UNDERSTANDING IMPOSTER SYNDROME — 30
THE POWER OF SELF-NARRATIVE — 34
THE CURSE OF COMPARISONS — 45

CHAPTER 3: THE BLOCK OF INDECISION — 57
THE ROOT OF INDECISION—AN INTOLERANCE FOR UNCERTAINTY — 60
INFORMATION OVERLOAD — 63
THE ANTIDOTE OF COMMITMENT — 70

CHAPTER 4: THE BLOCK OF FIXED MINDSET — 87
THE GIFT OF FAILING — 99

CHAPTER 5: THE BLOCK OF SELF-DECEPTION
111

HOW TO IDENTIFY SELF-DELUSION — 114
A LOOK AT DEFENSE MECHANISMS — 119

CHAPTER 6: THE BLOCK OF DISCOMFORT — 139

THE CURSE OF INAPPROPRIATE EXPECTATIONS — 146
THE RIGHT WAY AND THE EASY WAY ARE SELDOM THE SAME WAY — 150

CHAPTER 7: THE BLOCK OF CLOSE-MINDEDNESS
165

SUMMARY GUIDE — 185

Chapter 1: Turn Off Autopilot

Who is in control of your life?

This isn't a trick question. Think of all the things you have already done today, before sitting down to read these words in front of you. *Why* did you do any of them?

Intentional thinking is something that's easy to understand on an intellectual level, but harder to grasp when it comes to your actual lived experience, moment by moment, day by day. When we talk about intentional thinking, we're discussing an attitude, a way of being, a mindset and an approach to life that is characterized by control, focus, deliberation and will.

We could spend our time trying to control the events in our lives indirectly, but the real challenge is in reaching more deeply inside to control *ourselves* at a more fundamental level. When you change the way that you think, you also change the things you are thinking about. When you change the cognitive and attitudinal tools you're working with, you open up a whole new world of possibilities. Success, then, is a matter of perception and attitude before anything else.

Intentional thinking is easier to understand when we consider what it isn't. When we are not intentional, we act in passive, reactive ways, i.e. on "autopilot." We bounce around according to this or that whim, following every random distraction, never really aware of what we're doing any more than a leaf blowing in the wind. Or worse, we are at the mercy of our fears and weaknesses, or blindly following along with someone else's vision for our lives.

Often, the biggest insights in life, the most dramatic changes and the most lasting improvements come when we have the courage to act with intention and deliberation, actively steering our lives to where *we* want them to go. With conscious awareness, we use intention to focus our will like a laser, so that we can achieve the things we want.

Thinking with intention and deliberation is, almost by definition, not easy. It's certainly not obvious or automatic. But if you're reading this book, it's likely that you want to find ways to become better at it. Habit, old mental ruts, fears, assumptions and ego games all act to keep us where we are. We need discipline, honesty, awareness and a little self-compassion to challenge ourselves into reaching for something better—a life we deliberately and intentionally create for ourselves.

In the chapters that follow, we're going to be taking a close look at this most brilliant of all tools—the mind—and how to essentially program it for success. The contours of your world are determined by your attitude and mindset—and your conscious will can decide what attitude and mindset to cultivate. Intentional thinking is all about recognizing this power: to use your mind to control and optimize not only yourself, but the world you live in.

So, who is in control of your life?

Events *happen to us*. Accidents happen, random occurrences come our way. But our lived experience, the meaning we make for ourselves, our purpose and values—these things don't just happen to us. We *make* them happen. We decide how we respond to the events in our world. We decide who we are, what we want, and what we're going to do. We control our thoughts.

Right now, using nothing but the power of your conscious intention, *you can decide* to think positively, to focus on new possibilities, to face your fears, to pursue what really matters, to do the right thing, to create, to be successful... You can decide that tomorrow gets to be better than today. Isn't that the most mind-blowing privilege?

Be conscious.
Know yourself.
Identify mental blocks and work to remove them.
Release negativity.
Set a goal.
Achieve it.
Then do it all over again!

Whatever you choose to do with this unbelievable gift called your life, understand that it starts with something simple: your conscious awareness of your inborn right to think deliberately and with intention.

Luck certainly has something to do with success. And we'd be lying to ourselves if we said that privilege didn't have something to do with it, too. But no matter what happens, nothing can take away your ability to choose your response, to any of it. You are always in complete control of what goes on in your own head; always a sovereign, active agent—if you choose to be, that is!

Let's consider an example. A young graduate starts a new job. Unfortunately, there is some friction early on and the new employee quickly fails at an important task, which costs the company huge amounts of money. Rather than admit his mistake, though, the employee delays alerting management, stuck in indecision about what to do.

He can't stand knowing that he's messed up, and will be reprimanded by his employers—or worse. He tries to hide his mistake at first, and then, when he realizes he can't, he falls into a deep depression, knowing that people will question his competency. He starts to feel bad about himself, wishing he'd never taken the job.

He used to be at the top of his class! He's a genius, really. The more he thinks about it, the more he realizes it's his superiors who are in the wrong—it was *their* fault for giving him the assignment, their faulty software, their lack of oversight. When a meeting is held to discover what went wrong, the employee is almost hostile to the rest of his team. Seeing this, management are understandably not pleased, and things only get worse and worse for the employee.

The employee in this example has demonstrated all the pitfalls that come with a lack of conscious intention. Can you see his inability to take responsibility, to be flexible, to become consciously aware of his own role in the unfolding of his life?

First, his inability to bear discomfort leads him to delay admitting to his mistake. His fixed mindset and closed-mindedness cause him to react with stubbornness and indignation—rather than looking at the situation neutrally and asking what he can honestly do to improve the matter.

Because he is in a purely reactive and passive frame of mind, he wastes time in indecision, never quite knowing how to get out of his predicament. Finally, when he does act, he doesn't take ownership of his actions, and resorts to self-delusion and blame. Not only does this make it impossible for him to learn from his mistakes and genuinely become better at his work, but it alienates him from his colleagues and makes the consequences of his original mistake so much worse.

Throughout this example, the employee is merely reacting, responding unconsciously, always on the back foot. He never stops to ask himself, *What am I doing here? What is my role and my full scope of action? What do I want here and how I can achieve that?*

Consider how things could have played out differently. A new employee messes up at work, badly. They feel panicked at first but quickly realize that they have the power to shape the outcome, depending on how they choose to behave from that moment on. They look at all possible courses of action and realize that owning up to the mistake as quickly as possible will reflect the best on them.

Before they do this, though, they take a deep breath and realize that it's going to be uncomfortable. They are going to feel embarrassed and it's going to be unpleasant to have everyone angry at them. They may even be fired. But they are in control. Of themselves, what they say, and what they do.

They quickly own up to the mistake, and follow up with some realistic suggestions for what they can do to remedy the situation. They bear the anger and disappointment with humility, accepting full responsibility. They act immediately to do the right thing. They might have been a star student in university, but clearly, they have a lot to learn—so they commit to seeking the help of more experienced colleagues to learn a few things, even though this will take their ego down a peg.

Sure, the situation may be difficult for a time. But you can imagine that an employee who behaved this way after making a serious mistake has actually taken a bad situation and made something great from it, as management gets to see how they resolve conflict and act with maturity.

In this example, the employee *acts*, and doesn't just *react*.

He makes conscious decisions according to what's important, even if it's uncomfortable or unpleasant, and would be easier to blame someone else. He doesn't dissolve into self-doubt and delusion, but looks at the situation squarely and neutrally, trusting himself to handle things. He acts with decisiveness, flexibility, humility and an open-minded approach that guarantees he'll learn from the experience.

Here's what matters about these two examples: the event that started it all is exactly the same.

One employee can turn it into an embarrassing failure that he bitterly blames others for; the other can use it as a springboard to learn to become better at what he does. Each employee had *the same amount* of luck, opportunity and competency. They were faced with the *same* tricky situation. But the second one had something the first one didn't: a willingness to engage his intentional thinking and conscious awareness to behave in ways that ultimately served him best.

When people say "your thoughts create your reality," it's easy to imagine that they're talking about something quite mystical and far-out. But in fact, nothing could be more plain and obvious than the fact that your thoughts and attitude determine the kind of life you live.

There is no magic to it. It's simple: your thoughts determine your actions, and your actions shape your world. Your attitude creates your sense of possibility, your feeling of who you are and what you want (and deserve!), and these then impact the way you interpret events, respond to them, and take action of your own.

The world out there is what it is, but objective events get filtered through your own unique set of expectations, beliefs and mental blocks. We don't see the world as it is, but the world as it looks when passed through our particular mindset.

If we conduct ourselves with positivity, deliberate intention, compassionate awareness, flexibility, and so on, we will naturally find ourselves living in a different world than if we'd closed ourselves off in mindsets plagued with fear, negative habits, self-doubt, passivity and mindlessness.

Intentional thinking is your birthright. As a human being, you were *made* for conscious awareness, self-control, mastery, understanding and goal-directed action. But this is a skill set that doesn't come automatically—by its very nature, it has to be claimed deliberately. To develop and cultivate our intentional will, we only need to *choose* to do so. Nobody else can choose the path for us!

As we move through the chapters of this book, we'll be looking at everything that gets in the way of this natural, inbuilt capacity for self-determination and conscious, intentional thinking. If we can identify all the ways we don't want to think and behave, we can clear the path for all the ways we do. We'll look at all the mental blocks that trip us up, including the ones we saw in the examples above: self-doubt, indecision, self-delusion and closed-mindedness.

It can be difficult at first to build up a strong sense of intentional thinking. After all, how many of us were taught this skill at school, or see it modelled around us by people in our environments? Where do we even start? This is why it can be easier to begin with identifying what we want to avoid, and go from there.

In the chapters that follow, we'll use a simple and practical formula for identifying and tackling the mental blocks that threaten to get in the way of our empowered, intentional thinking. Whether the mental block is uncertainty, comparing yourself to others, or low self-esteem, these steps are a handy framework to help you untangle your limitations and build a robust mindset that will create real success.

Before we examine the steps in detail, though, be aware that from most of us, it can be difficult to honestly identify our mental blocks. Our most harmful and persistent blocks are those we don't even know we possess! For this reason, try to remember to practice a little open-mindedness and self-compassion as you attempt these steps on yourself later on—you may be surprised at what you find.

Intentional Thinking in Four Steps

Our first step is to UNCOVER the causes and roots of our mental blocks.

Let's return to our example of the first employee who messed up at work. This person chose not to own up to his mistake immediately, and instead defaulted to blame—why? Maybe a combination of his personality, upbringing, past experiences and personal values conspired to make him feel like it was simply not acceptable to fail, and that owning up to a mistake was a weakness to feel ashamed about.

Maybe this person feels they have no worth at all unless they are clever, always right, always on the ball. If this employee were to dig a little, they may find that some of their *core values* were intelligence, competence and prestige. Where did these core values come from?

Perhaps from a perfectionist parent, or training at an elite and ruthless university, or living in a culture that rewards ambition and punishes mediocrity. To uncover the hidden causes of your own mental blocks, you need only ask *why* again and again in the same way, until you reveal what is powering your assumptions, values and beliefs about yourself.

Ask:
What do I feel or think?
Why do I think/feel that way?
Who taught me this, or where did I first encounter this belief?
What associations do I have?
What life "rules" am I following?

What are the effects of this belief on my life?
Do I like how thinking this way makes me feel?

On reflection, the employee may discover that his unspoken belief is that "I am worthless if I fail." Looking closely can allow him to see something else: that these values and beliefs actually conflict with other convictions he holds. For example, he may see that in his life, refusing to acknowledge mistakes has cost him learning opportunities, and ironically made him *less* successful over time, and more likely to fail. He realizes that his mental blocks are actively hindering him from living the kind of life he wants.

The next step is to actually REMOVE the mental block.

Easier said than done! Be gentle on yourself—your mental blocks have probably been with you from childhood, and can be so fixed they seem like reality itself. This step takes time and patience, but the first thing you need to do is simply become aware of what you say to yourself, mentally, day in and day out.

At first, just listen as you talk to yourself. Pay attention to your inner monologue and hear the tone of voice you use, the phrases and words you keep returning to, the patterns. Become curious about where this perspective or interpretation comes from. Many people are often surprised to find that their inner voice is none other than that of a critical parent or teacher, or an amalgamation of other peoples' opinions.

Be curious and simply ask where thoughts and self-talk originates. When was the first time you felt or thought this way? Why?

The surest way to gradually start loosening the grip of a mental block is to challenge it once it appears. Don't simply take your own word for it—demand evidence. Do you *know* that such-and-such is the case, or have you simply told yourself so many times that you assume it's true?

Stopping to deliberately look at self-talk with a fresh eye invites in some intentional thinking. Our employee could notice himself saying, "you always mess up, you're a terrible person," and deliberately decide to pause to examine this claim.

Is it *really* true? No. He can find evidence that he has achieved many impressive things in life. True, he has made mistakes, but it's simply factually incorrect that he *always* messes up. He also argues with his self-belief—making mistakes doesn't make you a bad person. After all, haven't all his heroes made mistakes, too?

Challenging negative self-talk is not easy, but with repetition and time, you can gradually loosen automatic and unconscious beliefs that run on autopilot, sabotaging your success.

The third step is to REDUCE the mental block's power.

If you begin to pick at your mental blocks, you may start to notice something: you don't exactly *want* to be rid of them. This is because they exist for a reason. They serve a purpose. Sure, they may be limiting you in many ways, but chances are some of these mental blocks have their advantages, too.

For our employee, for example, his intolerance for failure may well inspire him to work extra hard, giving him grit and resilience, conveying an attitude of confidence and optimism. This makes tempering these mental blocks a little harder. The trick is to find moderation.

A useful analogy is to imagine that your life is a car, driving toward its destination (or off a cliff, if it's that kind of life!). Try to imagine that all your personality quirks, mental blocks, beliefs, values and so on are allowed in the car, but only as passengers— never as the driver.

So, our employee could acknowledge that his perfectionist streak is a part of him and has its uses at times, but ultimately it's his higher, conscious, intentional self that is driving the vehicle. He will not allow his fear of failure, in other words, to run the show. He will appreciate its contributions now and then, though.

The final step of the process is to TRANSFORM the mental block into something that is actually a valuable asset to your life. The thing is, when approached consciously and with intentional awareness, even our greatest flaws can be sources of meaning and growth for us.

For our employee, his perfectionism and inflexibility can be a stern teacher about the power of vulnerability, teaching him the importance of asking for help, staying humble, and the virtues of a growth mindset. His greatest insight could come from a real reversal of his core beliefs—i.e. that he is a valuable person and his efforts are worthwhile, no matter how many mistakes he makes. In fact, the more he experiences, the more he can grow. Being vulnerable and admitting imperfection or ignorance ironically makes him stronger.

Identifying mental blocks is a necessary first step, but we really grow and change when we take conscious, focused *action*. If you're afraid and uncertain, ask for help. If you're stuck comparing yourself to others, decide to reach out and compliment someone you admire, and then take one step toward achieving your own goals. If you know that you are usually triggered by tight deadlines, plan accordingly and take action to work around your limitations.

Self-doubt, uncertainty, negative self-talk, and similar issues are not problems in themselves. When you become aware of them, however, you can take control and start to act toward something better. Look at your mind for what it is: something that can be reprogrammed, improved, enhanced. It can grow and adapt. *You can be better.*

These four steps of **uncover, remove, reduce and transform** actually overlap in reality, and are never really finished. It took a lifetime to program your personal mental blocks, and it will take time to gradually replace them with something better. We'll be returning to these four straightforward steps again and again in the chapters that follow, and that's simply because they work, no matter what mental blocks we're talking about.

Once you get the hang of removing the obstacles between you and conscious, intentional thinking, then the sky really is the limit.

The takeaway:

- Intentional thinking is the conscious, willful control of your own thought processes so that you can actively direct your own life toward success. By thinking intentionally, you determine your own place in the world and gain control of your daily life.
- Thoughts have power, and our attitude and mindset create our world. The worst tragedies can be overcome if you have the right approach and use intentional thinking to respond to challenges in the most growth-oriented manner possible.
- Passivity, apathy, reactivity, failing to take responsibility, and failing to own our agency means we never achieve our goals, or even identify them in the first place. We are at the mercy of fleeting whims, fears, or the wishes of others, and cannot follow our own true path or purpose.
- Mental blocks can impede our ability to think intentionally. Examples are self-deception, closed-mindedness,

fear of discomfort, indecisiveness and self-doubt. Given how essential our thoughts are to who we are, what we do, how we perceive the world around us and exist in it, and so on, these mental blocks need to be carefully replaced with healthier modes of thinking.

- Throughout this book, we'll use the formula "uncover, remove, reduce, and transform" to address these mental blocks and develop intentional thinking. We can tackle mental blocks by uncovering their cause, removing them by challenging our self-talk, beliefs and assumptions, reducing the impact these blocks have on our lives, and slowly transforming this part of ourselves into something beneficial.

Chapter 2: The Block of Self-Doubt

Let's dive in with a particularly common mental block that you'll probably recognize in yourself: the block of self-doubt. You likely don't need a long explanation of what self-doubt is—most of us have experienced feelings of inadequacy in life, or have felt occasionally that we are not smart enough, successful enough, fit enough, attractive enough... really, that *we are not enough*, period.

This belief can be so fixed within us that it can persist even in the face of obvious evidence to the contrary. Whether we lack faith in our own abilities or worth because of the way we were raised, our personalities, unrealistic cultural standards, or our life experiences and relationships with others, self-doubt can be strange in that it often appears to have nothing to do with objective reality.

Understanding Imposter Syndrome

The classic example of someone suffering from so-called imposter syndrome is the overachiever who excels at their job and yet has such low self-esteem that they are convinced their success has all been a horrible mistake, a bit of luck or a fluke. They live with the gnawing suspicion that one day they'll be found out for the frauds they really are, and their accolades will be stripped and given to someone else who *really* deserves them.

Feeling like an imposter when you achieve success is explained by looking at underlying beliefs, which are powerful enough to warp our perception of reality. The belief is, "I'm a bad/useless/stupid/unworthy person." When something in the "real world" happens to directly challenge that belief (i.e. you're promoted or win an award), you have two choices: change the belief to match reality… or hold on to the belief even more tightly.

The only way to make the belief "I'm a useless person" fit in a world where you have literally won an award for excellence is to tell yourself a story where the award was simply given in error. In other words, you *appear* to be a successful person, but it's merely a temporary illusion. Not only that, but when other people realize just how useless you really are, it's going to be extra humiliating…

The prevalence of imposter syndrome is yet more evidence for the premise we began our book with: your thoughts create your experience. So much so that when thoughts and reality are pitted against one another, our thoughts can actually win out, shaping a world for us that is wholly different from what others would call objective reality.

Take a moment to really think about this: your thoughts are so powerful at creating your felt experience that they can even work against plain, objective reality. Isn't that a power worth learning to use correctly?

If you often find yourself feeling like a fraud who's one day going to be found out, try to consider how this perception may be actively limiting you and your success and well-being. Being your own "anti-cheerleader" means you constantly downplay your achievements, amplify your weaknesses and interpret events in their worst possible light.

Thinking this way narrows your sense of possibility, stunts your creativity and keeps you acting small. Worst of all, imposter syndrome can have a nasty habit of becoming a self-fulfilling prophecy—if you think, feel and behave as though you are unworthy and undeserving, it won't take external reality long to catch up with your assessment and start reflecting that back to you. Not such a great outcome for someone who may have considered themselves a "perfectionist"!

Perfectionism is not the only attitude that will predispose you to imposter syndrome, and indirectly block your ability to live an intentional, conscious life. Consider the following beliefs or thoughts:

- I have to be an overachiever and do it all perfectly
- I have to do it all on my own—asking for help is unacceptable
- I have to find this challenge easy and natural, I need talent/genius
- I have to be an expert, I have to know everything

Though certain cultures, work environments or even families may hold these mindsets as ideal, the truth is that they're fragile, hard to live up to, and seldom predict actual success. Instead, the expectation that comes with such a heavy need to perform actually creates anxiety.

This anxiety can potentially push a person to procrastinate, rushing through the task at the last moment. If they are praised, this praise is written off—after all, they didn't really "earn" it, it was just dumb luck, and nobody saw how frantic they were to just barely complete the task.

On the other hand, the anxiety can push a person to over-prepare, and work extra hard to complete the project. In this case, praise can also be interpreted through the filter of self-doubt—one could reason that they only succeeded by virtue of superhuman effort, whereas others who are naturally gifted achieve the same result with much less effort.

Is imposter syndrome more prevalent in women than men? The concept was originally used to explore this phenomenon in high-achieving women, but the fact is, anyone can experience self-doubt. Of course, things can get complicated when we add gender or ethnicity into the mix. There's no doubt that some people feel like frauds in their careers precisely because they live in a world that confirms this belief!

Thoughts create our experience, but unfortunately, we live in a world populated by *other peoples'* thoughts, beliefs, and actions, which inevitably impact our own. This brings us to an important mechanism through which thoughts actually create our world: stories.

The Power of Self-Narrative

The felt *emotion* of shame, low self-worth or low confidence expresses itself in narrative form. It is revealed in the mental stories we tell ourselves, and consequently others. How we feel about ourselves, our deepest held beliefs and values take shape as thoughts and ideas that link together into complex narratives about who we are, what we do, why we do it, and so on.

In a sense, every one of the mental blocks we'll explore in the chapters that follow is a kind of story we tell ourselves (and believe!). Self-talk is not just what happens moment by moment in daily life (for example, thinking "I'm such an idiot" when you drop something); it's the persistent pattern of thoughts and stories that make up nothing less than your complete identity.

When we have self-doubt, it's almost always because we have gotten carried away with a narrative in which we play the character that is inept, bad, useless, wrong. This could have originally come from being judged and criticized harshly by others, but it could equally appear to have no single root cause. Whatever the case, someone with self-doubt has told themselves a particular story so often that they've come to believe it, not even realizing it's a story anymore, but assuming they are simply encountering reality.

For the person with imposter syndrome, for example, the narrative of "you are a loser" trumps all. It becomes a lens through which every event is interpreted, but it's also a filter that works the other way around, altering the words you use, how you carry yourself, the actions you take.

The trick is that if your self-narrative is poor, you're essentially locking yourself into patterns of behavior that actively limit and undermine your real potential. When you buy into negative self-talk and the story you tell about yourself, you stop behaving spontaneously and authentically. Instead, *you act according to the role you have already assigned yourself.*

If you truly believe that you are incompetent and stupid, why would you ever try out something new, take a chance, or volunteer your opinion? For that matter, why would you bother asserting your boundaries or protecting yourself against things that are bad for you?

If you already "know" that you're a failure, then there's no need to start a new project, learn anything new, go an adventure, risk falling in love, challenge yourself or speak up and make your voice heard—after all, you already know how the story ends. In your narrative, you are and always will be a loser. Everything that has to do with your not being a loser is simply invisible to you.

When you have imposter syndrome, or when you're in the grips of low self-esteem and extreme self-doubt, your vision narrows till you see only what you falsely believe is a threat: being found out, failing, being uncomfortable.

In reality, the greatest risk to having self-doubt is not in what you might do (i.e. fail) but in what you might never risk doing (i.e. succeed). Another way of putting this is that a poor self-narrative has an extremely high *opportunity cost*. When you work hard to convince yourself of a negative narrative, you are actively turning away from real opportunities to get what you want.

You don't see promising opportunities when they emerge, and so you never grab them when you can. You don't hear compliments, and so never enjoy them, or let them soak in and become part of your self-concept. You don't enjoy your life as it's happening, or appreciate the many wonderful things you have, because you're tangled up in a negative story that constantly takes you out of the present.

You don't take risks and so you don't reap those rewards. You essentially talk yourself into a corner, staying in your comfort zone while your amazing, fulfilling and exciting life goes unlived somewhere out there.

Humans have a cognitive bias where we tend to focus on the risks of what we could lose in the moment by acting, and forget to weigh up what we lose in future by *not* acting. In the moment, the self-doubt narrative seems really convincing. It's a little voice that's so easy to obey. But in reality, this is a mental block that only saps our power and keeps us thinking small.

Sometimes, we choose to stick to these negative stories because they give us a way out of putting in the effort we need to improve as people. A positive story requires constant effort and reassurance to maintain, whereas negative stories absolve us of that burden. If we're a fraud or an imposter, why would we bother doing anything? We need not put in the work to achieve our goals, we need not worry about successes and failures because the end result is always disappointment. But if you truly believe that you are a capable individual, you're susceptible to fluctuating fortunes unless you can practice self-compassion and positive self-talk. Though more arduous, ultimately this is the approach that will improve your self-esteem, give you a sense of agency, and make you feel in control of your life.

How to change your self-defeating narratives

We don't change our mental stories with more judgment, shame, self-criticism, or by heaping on yet more perfectionism. We change them with patience and *self-compassion.*

Self-compassion is a brilliant antidote to some of the mindsets we've explored above because it basically tells us that yes, sometimes human beings experience pain and suffering, and sometimes they fail and behave poorly, but all of this is a part of the normal human experience, and doesn't mean any of us is less worthy of love.

Self-compassion doesn't mean we condone unacceptable aspects of life or behavior or suddenly lack standards for ourselves. Rather, it's about shifting the attitude we hold when we regard ourselves and the lives we live. Can we go a little easier on ourselves? Can we do what needs to be done, but with a spirit of care, kindness and good humor?

Adopting an attitude of self-compassion has real, concrete benefits. When you deliberately act to soothe and calm yourself, to refrain from shame and self-criticism, you instantly dial down your body's stress response. Your mental health improves, you can think a little more clearly and you may even find your relationships feel more harmonious.

When you're constantly on high alert and unconsciously telling your body that it's under threat, you flood your system with stress hormones and act out of fear—not a good place to cultivate conscious, intentional thinking.

Intentional thinking takes a little time. It needs a quiet, peaceful moment to thoughtfully consider all aspects of a situation at hand, to become fully aware of what's occurring, to really feel what's taking place internally in body and mind, and to contemplate. None of this can be done if you're constantly stressed and strung out, rushing from one thing to the next, reacting to one minor crisis after another. And it's especially not possible when a great chunk of your mental processing power is being wasted on thoughts like, *Don't mess this up again, you stupid idiot.*

When we talk about mental narratives and stories, it's easy to imagine we're talking merely about *cognition*, or the *intellectual content* of a story. But if we hope to make lasting and genuine changes to our self-concept, we need to dig a little deeper, and look at the *emotional content* of the stories we tell ourselves.

Our stories can take millions of different forms, and be told in countless words and phrases. But ignore the words, the layout and story itself, and try to become aware of what it *feels* like to tell yourself a particular story. This is the beating heart of your self-narrative, and this is where you need to focus your attention if you hope to change it.

Try a meditation practice where you deliberately bring a little compassion to limiting self-beliefs. Start by becoming aware of how you talk to yourself, and how that feels. Try to put words or symbols on the emotion behind the narrative, but don't lose sight of the fact that the symbols and thoughts are merely vehicles to carry lived, felt experience.

Now, sit with these feelings. Don't try to avoid them, cover them, argue with them or get angry with them. Just become curious about what they are. Even doing this is starting to flex your conscious, intentional awareness. Simply notice the feelings, and the thoughts they inspire, rather than automatically and unconsciously allowing yourself to be compelled by them.

Accept them fully as a part of you, as part of your experience, without clinging but also without rejecting. Imagine, if you like, that some of these difficult emotions are simply guests you've invited to dinner. Invite them in and hear what they have to say.

You might like to visualize a warm, golden light to represent your accepting self-compassion—imagine this warm light encompassing all parts of yourself, even the more difficult and painful ones. Try reciting a mantra or affirmation that reinforces your commitment to be kind to yourself:

"I know who I am, and I am enough."
"I am worthy, right here, right now, just as I am."
"I can do this."
"I treat myself with kindness, love and respect."
"I forgive myself."
"I matter."
"It's OK to feel how I feel."

With time, you can start to truly believe this alternative narrative over the negative one—a new narrative in which you're a human, doing your best, who deserves patience and understanding as you navigate this sometimes crazy experience called life.

Practicing self-compassion doesn't mean you can't still work really hard, have ambitious dreams for yourself, feel disappointed, confused, or hurt—it just means that you do all these things while acting as your own best friend and ally. It means you deliberately and consciously choose to focus on compassion, gentleness, care and kindness.

Self-compassion bypasses all the distracting stories and narratives we tell ourselves and gets to the actual root of the matter: our core emotional experience. When we work at this level, we see our limiting and unhelpful self-beliefs start to fall away. We notice how bad it feels to hate ourselves, to judge ourselves or be unkind to ourselves when we are scared, confused or sad.

With repeated self-compassion, we can start to remove the damaging mental block of self-doubt and replace it with self-belief. In this frame of mind, we derive our sense of worth *internally*, and know that it isn't the end of the world to fail. We trust our abilities, forgive our mistakes, and yes, love ourselves.

The Curse of Comparisons

Self-compassion is a general approach to combating self-doubt, and something that each of us would do well to practice every day. But let's zoom in a little and consider some more detailed, practical ways of tackling feelings of inferiority or low self-esteem. Let's return to our process of **uncover, remove, reduce and transform** and see how someone might use these tactics to dismantle self-doubt narratives in real life.

Let's imagine someone who is in the grips of the curse called "making comparisons." You know how this goes: you feel pretty OK about yourself until you look at someone else's achievements, and you're suddenly overwhelmed by a crushing sense of failure and inadequacy.

Social media almost seems like a machine designed to make this painful comparison game as efficient as possible—we are bombarded with images of people living amazing lives, and we feel worthless in comparison.

Imagine a woman who regularly sees pictures of her friends and acquaintances going on expensive holidays to exotic locations, succeeding at work and living the high life, bragging about their workouts, their glittering social lives, showing off their beautiful homes, their beautiful families, their beautiful selves... it's enough to make anyone feel like their life is a total failure by comparison.

The narrative goes like this: "Look at all those awesome people out there. Everyone else is living their best life and I'm just here on the sofa in my pajamas, with my life passing me by. Compared to them I'm so fat/poor/ugly/stupid..."

Can you immediately see how this thought process can totally undermine intentional and conscious thinking? Comparing yourself to others does a few things (none of them good): it makes you feel awful, it distorts your perceptions, and most importantly, it disempowers you.

Comparisons are disempowering because they place your self-worth and identify *outside* of yourself, rather than inside. Rather than proactively deciding what's important to you based on your own desires and values, you look to others and respond passively to what you see, behaving out of fear and a sense of lack rather than being genuinely motivated and inspired to act with passion.

A narrative in which you compare yourself to others is particularly damaging for a few reasons:

- You're not basing your comparisons on accurate data, anyway. Social media is, as they say, the "highlights reel" and curated to contain only the best bits. You don't see your idols sitting on the sofa feeling like failures themselves!

- You're robbing yourself of the opportunity to enjoy your life, right now, as it is. Whenever you compare the current situation with some hypothetical better one, you devalue what is, and set yourself up for perpetual dissatisfaction. The truth is, there's always going to be someone smarter, more attractive, and wealthier than you. Does it make sense to allow this fact to drain your life of any potential joy you could experience from being just as you are?
- You're disregarding your own uniqueness. Sure, some success can be measured quantitatively, i.e. how much money we earn. But most things in life, the things that truly matter, are not so easily comparable in the first place. How can you really measure happiness? Fulfilment? Purpose? When you rank yourself against others, you do *everyone* a disservice, because you're ignoring how everyone is 100 percent a unique individual.

- You're missing the opportunity to be inspired by those who could teach you something, or become your mentors. When you compare yourself to others, you cultivate jealousy, envy and resentment. What would happen instead if you celebrated others' achievements, complimented them and sought their advice and help in your own life? Instead of being passively jealous, what if you were inspired to be the best version of yourself?

The woman in our example could begin by **uncovering** the root of her feelings of self-doubt, and why she feels compelled to compare herself to others. She may find that she was taught from a young age to value physical appearances and external markers of status and success, and may also discover a simpler fact that daily social media use is bad for her mental health.

She can look at these facts with compassion, and forgive herself for getting a little addicted to social media but also develop a kind concern about the core beliefs of low self-worth she may be holding.

Next, she could become aware of these thoughts and feelings when they emerge, and seek to **remove** them. For example, every time she notices herself feeling bad about her life, she can reach for a gratitude journal and write down three things she is grateful for. She could compile a list of good qualities she knows she has and read them to herself when in self-doubt.

She can repeat the mantra "I am enough" over and over again, focusing on the feeling and not just the words. She could simply step away from the screen and go for a walk, reminding herself of her ultimate values and life purpose.

In time, she can **reduce** her self-doubt mental block, and the compulsion to compare herself to others will diminish. She realizes that it's OK to be impressed and inspired by others, but she commits to using this impulse to look more honestly into herself: are there any dreams that she has been ignoring? What does her envy for others say about her own life purpose? Rather than getting lost in shame and self-hate, can she find ways to express her unique self, and shine a little more?

In this way, comparisons and self-doubt are **transformed**. Awareness and conscious intention change everything. The great thing about intentional thinking is that it's somehow both a cause and an effect of a well-lived life. The more we engage in purpose-driven, decisive action powered by our own values, the easier it is to feel confident in ourselves and set up a "virtuous cycle."

This woman could put away her phone and ask herself honestly what she wants to achieve in life, then go out and start taking actions toward that goal. This boosts her self-esteem and strengthens her internal locus of control, both of which make it so that she genuinely cares less and less about what other people are doing. Rather than passively responding to images of other peoples' lives, she is out there actively creating her own.

Practical ways to have less self-doubt and more confidence in yourself

Act the part
Dress nicely. Spend time on grooming, taking care of your appearance, getting a nice haircut, wearing fragrance, and standing up straight, shoulders back and chin up. No, looking good isn't the answer to a low self-esteem, but it does subtly communicate the message to your unconscious mind: you are worth the effort. You are valuable and need to be taken care of. If you treat yourself, your body and your appearance with disrespect or disinterest, you're conveying to others that you're not valuable. It might feel vain at first, but eventually you'll notice the impact your clothes and grooming can have on your confidence and self-esteem. Similarly, seeing that you value yourself will make other people treat you as important as well.

Cultivate the right kind of mental bias
Deliberately seek the generous, positive interpretation of events. It may sound cheesy, but the more you smile, the kinder you feel. The more you put an optimistic spin on things, the more you'll start to believe it and act accordingly. Your mom was kind of right when she told you, "If you haven't got something nice to say, then

don't say anything." Watch your language: get rid of harsh words, swearing, criticism, judgment. Replace "can't" with "won't" or talk about "challenges" rather than "problems." Remember, your mind is a program. Input positivity, and it'll put out positivity as well. Find the silver lining in every negative outcome—there will always be one waiting to be discovered.

Slow down and go small
There's no rush. Talk more slowly and clearly, and give yourself the opportunity to think things over—plus you'll present yourself as more deliberate and trustworthy to others. Don't stress about making quantum leaps. Just make one small change and stick to it for the long term, then make another. Pace yourself. Working consistently on small goals that build over time is more powerful—and achievable and sustainable—than making impressive improvements all in one go. Focus on small, manageable habits: the little things add up more quickly than you realize.

The takeaway:

- The mental block of self-doubt can show up in the form of imposter syndrome, where we choose to listen to our negative self-belief rather than the objective evidence of our success. We could be the best at what we do, yet some of us suffer from a nagging suspicion that our successes are a result of pure chance, and that fate, not merit, has made us successful. As such, you might fear being discovered for the incompetent self you really are.
- The narrative of a person suffering from imposter syndrome is just one of many that we could tell ourselves. Our core self-beliefs inform the stories we tell about ourselves—and these narratives often work against us.
- We can change our core beliefs by slowly reworking our self-narratives. We can do this by accepting our negative emotions with self-compassion and curiosity, before we gently rewrite our stories. Avoid the temptation to compare yourself to others, especially if you are active on social media. Places like Instagram

make you feel bad about your life because you're constantly subjected to a barrage of updates with all of your friends posting about their successes, vacations, etc. However, it is important to remember that nobody posts their failures and dull moments, and that their reality is likely to be much closer to your own.
- When we slow down and become curious about why we feel as we do, we can start to reduce, remove and transform negative self-belief into a feeling of self-love and high self-esteem. Other practical ways to reinforce a confident mindset are to dress the part and spend time grooming yourself the way someone who values themselves would, and cultivate the right mental biases which look for the silver lining in every negative outcome.

Chapter 3: The Block of Indecision

An enormous mental block exists whenever we hesitate too much and fail to act, thus missing out on opportunities. Like perfectionism, getting trapped in "analysis paralysis" is something that stems from an ordinarily useful human tendency. It's only natural to want to delay making a choice until you have as much information as possible, so you can make the best decision. But this tactic can easily go too far!

Of course, it's true that taking the time to critically assess your full scope of possible action means you're better positioned to choose the right way forward. However, the fact is that we can only ever *approximate* the perfect decision—it's not practically possible to act with complete certainty. Good decision-making is something we can do to a point, beyond which we have to acknowledge that some things are simply out of our hands.

You'll know that indecision is a serious block for you if you often find yourself feeling unable to commit fully to any one path, delaying the moment of choice till the last minute, often incurring costs in the process. The costs of not taking the leap from *thought into action* can be high—and yet we seldom factor these costs in when we're dawdling and scrutinizing the situation endlessly.

Being indecisive simply feels awful. The longer you remain unsettled, the higher your anxiety, and the greater the stakes. The more you delay, the bigger the choice actually seems to become, and the more you're aware of not having chosen—a vicious cycle. We can lose all sense of proportion when it comes to assessing how important any one decision actually is… and risk ignoring the things that really do matter.

Indecisiveness has a way of becoming a self-fulfilling prophecy, too. For example, you believe a decision is super important, so you take your time trying to make it. You don't want to choose the wrong thing and mess up! But in taking so long to find the perfect way forward, the decision goes stale and you miss out, literally losing opportunities or defaulting to how things were before. Your indecision acts to bring about the very thing you were afraid of.

Analysis paralysis is just that: the paralyzed feeling of unpicking a situation to such a degree you have no idea what to do anymore, and no ability left to act. In this sense, someone who analyzes things *less* has a greater chance of success simply because they actually get things done. A task completed moderately well is always more valuable than grand visions that never materialize.

Sure, people who take a risk now and then may have a marginally higher chance of making the wrong decision, but they didn't waste time figuring that out. In fact, they may be able to fix their mistake and choose again several times over before the paralyzed person has even managed to take a single action.

The Root of Indecision—An Intolerance for Uncertainty

Even if you're unaware of it, your brain is constantly appraising and assessing the environment around you, making predictions, drawing conclusions, inferring from incomplete data and filling in the gaps given the existence of time constraints and limited resources.

Perfectionism and indecision are fed primarily by fear—a fear of the unknown. In many ways this is a remnant of our early days as hunter-gatherers, when an unknown factor could easily result in death. As such, from an evolutionary perspective, the fear of the unknown has kept us alive for centuries and millennia. Even in the modern day, the unknown can pose existential threats, but these are much less pronounced. Primarily, it exacerbates our fear of missing out, which is a form of social anxiety that disproportionately affects some people over others. This could be the fear of missing out on better alternatives, better outcomes resulting from particular actions, etc.

When we analyze the world, we are seeking to understand it. By cognitively grasping the details of the world we inhabit, we enjoy a degree of mastery over it. We orient ourselves in our surroundings and can structure and organize our lives. A lot of this rests on our assessment of probabilities and likelihoods.

We decide what actions to take based on our understanding of the risks and benefits involved. We don't *know* the sun will rise tomorrow, for example, but we're fairly certain it will. We trust most people not to rob us, we assume that the box we bought at the supermarket contains what it says it does, and on a grander scale, we trust that if we work hard we'll probably succeed. We build our lives and actions around what we know, trust and can depend upon.

Anything new entering our worlds can be perceived as threatening, simply because of this fact: we don't yet understand it. We don't know where it fits into our world. It could be a good thing, but it could also be terrible. Until we know, we behave cautiously. And the way we can move from ignorance to understanding (and to the comfort of being certain again) is to gather more data.

In an ideal world, we'd approach the unknown with a curious, open mind, gather data and learn more about it, and move on with life. But what happens if we get stuck in the data-gathering stage? What about realizing that we can never actually learn *everything* there is to know about a phenomenon, can never predict anything with 100 percent accuracy, and can never have perfect understanding?

At some point, we have to act, even when we're a little unsure.

Here we see that an intolerance for uncertainty is closely connected with perfectionism—the fear of the unknown causing us anxiety that we hope to relieve by somehow making the "perfect" decision. This is a question of trust and risk. Are we able to act despite never really having complete knowledge? Can we take the risk even though we can never guarantee what the outcome will be?

It's normal to be fearful of doing the wrong thing, but when this impulse gets in the way of us doing *any*thing at all, then it's a problem. The cost is that we forfeit our natural intentional thinking capacity, and start to behave as though the world is one giant threat that we should dedicate ourselves to mitigating at all times. Not exactly the attitude of success!

We can improve on our decision-making process, but we can never be completely perfect. Every time we act, we take risks. The only way to guarantee never incurring any risk at all is to simply never act—to never live at all (which, in a way, is the logical outcome of analysis paralysis!).

Information Overload

There are emotional reasons behind indecision—fear of change or intolerance of imperfection and uncertainty—but there are also cognitive ones. The fact is that modern humans have access to more information than ever before. It's no exaggeration to say that with some avenues of knowledge, no single human being could absorb all the available data in one lifetime.

This makes it difficult to follow the usual algorithm of "seek all the info and then make an informed decision." It becomes a question, naturally, of when to stop.

We can understand the illusion of completeness in the same way as we understand the illusion of total certainty or total security. The fact is that none of us ever acts with all available information. Life would be very boring if that were the case!

Since we are imperfect organisms who don't come into the world complete and finished, we inevitably need to learn and acquire knowledge during the course of life. And this means that we necessarily have to act even though we're uncertain, or don't really know what we're dealing with. If life wasn't this way, there would be no such thing as learning at all.

Endlessly combing through information may feel like it soothes a certain kind of anxiety, but it doesn't really help after a point. Combine this with the self-doubt we explored in the previous chapter, and this drive to gather more and more information could actually end up as self-sabotage.

To avoid the overwhelm that comes with living in a hyper-connected, data-saturated world, we need to have a clear-cut strategy before we start. We need to know what problem we are trying to solve, and what information *specifically* we are looking for.

Gathering information should not be a passive process, but a guided, deliberate one. Without structuring our search, we have nothing to direct us and risk getting bogged down in irrelevant detail.

If we're shopping for a new car, deciding where to go on holiday, planning a wedding, wondering what to wear to that interview or even mulling over a potential break-up, we need to understand from the outset that *the final goal is always action*. To take the first example, what exactly do you need to know before buying a car? That depends on what you're looking for. Size, type of gear, ground clearance, price, etc., are all elements you can consider. These act as filters and narrow down the options available to you. Once you have a sufficiently small list, your choice is not likely to matter much since all of them fit the criteria you've set. In other words, the opportunity cost is very low. By narrowing your choices in this manner, you can ease the burden of deciding between too many alternatives.

To take that final step of choosing, try to reframe what an effective, successful person looks like: not someone who never makes a mistake or experiences uncertainty, but someone who courageously acts with the best of their knowledge, and owns those actions.

The happy truth is that we can always learn, adjust our course or make changes even after we act. It's not as though the single decision in front of us is the be-all-and-end-all in life; we can continuously fine-tune, enjoying the process of learning rather than experiencing it as a deviation from perfection. It can be difficult at first, but practice being OK with "good enough" decisions. As they say, "Finished is better than perfect"!

In fact, you might find some solace in the Japanese concept of *wabi sabi*, which teaches us that nothing lasts, nothing is perfect, and nothing is finished. We live in an organic universe that is constantly flowing, moving, changing, growing. Everything is in process, and part of a dynamic cycle. Can we find beauty in imperfection, and joy in incomplete understanding?

If information overload is something you struggle with often, you may also find it helpful to deliberately narrow down your field of perception. This may seem like heresy to those of us who grew up in the digital age, but try to adopt a simpler, slower life. Embrace a little minimalism and do a "digital detox" once in a while where you commit to not flooding your brain with endless stimuli on screens all day.

The mindset of indecision frequently comes down not only to fear and lack of belief in our own competence, but also to overstimulation, confusion and too much choice. The "paradox of choice" acknowledges that sometimes, more options actually leads to more anxiety, hesitation, and dissatisfaction with whatever you do end up choosing.

And the bad thing you worry might happen once you make a decision? It may not be as bad as you're imagining. Psychologists have found that human beings are actually rather good at justifying the decisions they've made *after* the fact, whatever the decision is.

Think about that: once a decision is made and becomes real and a part of your life, you're quite likely to roll with it, since the alternatives are no longer available to you. The door of other options closing can paradoxically be the very thing that makes you feel content and satisfied with the reality you find yourself faced with. It may seem strange, but sometimes, making *any* decision is fine, and often something you'll be happy with regardless.

Have you ever noticed how many parents say things like, "We didn't plan on the pregnancy, but we couldn't be happier now"? Before you take action, you may have an overinflated sense of how important your decision is, or what it means for your happiness and success. You don't get to see what life feels like on the other side of that decision until you actually make it—and then you may discover that it's not such a big deal after all.

When you're bombarded with choices, you may feel that your decision holds more weight than it really does. Think about how modern people can swipe past hundreds of potential partners on dating apps and still feel utterly alone, and yet presumably our ancestors reliably found mates when they lived in small groups of one or two hundred people.

If you suffer from indecision, scale things back for yourself. Deliberately give yourself less choice—if you know you only have a choice between meal A or meal B, you spare yourself the agony of weighing up the pros and cons of everything on the menu. You just have your meal and get on with life! Pretty simple.

But if you *do* make a bad decision, that's cool too. It means you've earned some *valuable* data (as opposed to just data). Use this to guide your next decision. This little nugget of information is incredibly valuable to you. After all, you can spend hours trying to *guess* how a certain choice will play out... or you can simply try it, see what happens, and know for sure.

The Antidote of Commitment

The above applies to simple things like choosing what to order at a restaurant, but what about bigger life decisions? How can we use the best of our critical thinking skills without becoming bogged down in over-analysis?

This is a book about conscious intention and will, so we'll start there. Let's reclaim our cognitive powers to use *deliberately*, rather than letting our brains get carried away with distracting or distressing stimuli. When we act from our own personal agency, we start from within. Once we clarify our own will and intention, then we can turn outwards to take in data and process it, according to our needs. This is different form merely reacting to information overload and external pressure.

To loosen the mental block of indecision and allow more intentional thinking to guide our actions, we need to connect more deeply to our *values*. Sometimes, indecisiveness is a symptom of not really knowing what you want. And this in turn is a sign that your actions are not being guided by your bigger purpose or sincerely held values and beliefs.

Values, purpose and beliefs may sound like insubstantial things, but in truth they are incredibly energizing in a practical sense—when we know exactly what we value, we know what we want and can focus on getting it. It's like turbo-charging our will. Our will can do almost anything, but it doesn't function without a *why*. If your reason, purpose, motivation and actions aren't properly aligned, you'll often find yourself unable to act decisively.

Maybe you can't reach a decision because unconsciously, you know that *none* of the options actually leads where you want. Maybe you can't decide because you're lacking the inspiration and desire that come with a real purpose. When we have goals that speak to our values, we are clear about who we are and what we are doing. We may feel nervous, but we are seldom half-hearted or hesitant. In fact, we typically *can't wait* to act.

The block of indecision can often be removed if we take the time to sort out what we really care about, and why, and what we're trying to actually achieve in this life. Once we've determined our values, we should work hard to align our actions with our goals. It's simple: are our choices working to bring us closer to who we want to become, or further away?

The great thing about centering your values is that it helps you to act even if you haven't clarified your specific goals yet. Focus instead on what kind of a person you become by holding your values, then use this to inspire your choices. Do you value being a person who always acts with compassion and kindness? Are you the kind of person who always prioritizes their creativity? Are you an independent thinker who wants to arrive at their own conclusions about life?

Even without any particular goals, you can use your values to guide actions, instantly cut down on the noise and get to the heart of what you really care about. Knowing who you are and what you value helps you tune out data that doesn't matter—for example, other people's opinions or information that you cannot change.

Commitment is then being able to say, "I pour all of my energy into this chosen goal, which means the most to me." You are not left wondering if the other path was the better choice. You are too focused on the path you have chosen.

Finally, another aspect of information overload and indecisiveness is one you might not have considered: the issue of time. Have you ever sat down with a difficult decision and gotten yourself twisted in mental knots because of what's already happened, what might happen if this or that comes to be, what could happen, what *should* have happened differently in the past, and what might have happened in the future if that had occurred…

In all this, you can overlook one important thing: what is happening right now in the present. We certainly need to consider the past and the future in our decision-making—but we need to remember that the present trumps this data, since in all cases the present is the only thing we have any real power to change, right now.

The past is completed and cannot be changed, and the future hasn't arrived yet, and we cannot alter it no matter how much we stew over possibilities and potentialities now. Being overly influenced by the past or the future actually muzzles our power of intention, because this is a power that acts in the here and now. It cannot work anywhere other than the present.

It's also disempowering to gather endless data that actually may have little bearing on the situation in front of you right now. In fact, dwelling on the past or future can be a sign of harmful self-narratives that are working against you.

The mindset of indecisiveness is one that gets bogged down in information and endless stories that don't go anywhere. The only way out, the only way to inhabit your conscious will and intention, is to focus on your values, in the present, and gather only what data is necessary, with a deliberate intention to *act*.

As an example, a woman may find herself unable to decide whether it's a good idea to up and move to another city for a job offer. She stresses herself out endlessly by "researching" the new city, her job, and so on. She confuses herself by asking more and more people for their opinions and drawing up endless pros and cons tables, but never really asks *what she wants.*

Uncover: With introspection, she may discover that her self-doubt and low self-worth is telling her that if she messes up, she will never get another good opportunity again, and so she has to optimize her choices now or risk being unhappy forever. (Yikes! That's a lot of pressure.)

Remove: She can challenge these beliefs and remind herself that there are other jobs, and plenty of options—it's not just A or B. She is free to act according to her values. She reminds herself to take her time, and see whether the new move actually fits the goals she has for herself.

Reduce: Knowing that she can never really predict what living in the new city would be like, she asks for a little time to explore the city beforehand before she makes her decision. Her caution is not wrong, but it can be better channeled into taking action that will empower her rather than make her more anxious.

Transform: Seeing how effectively she is able to pick apart the decision at hand, the woman can also appreciate that she is very detail oriented and organized. In a way, this is something that can bolster her self-esteem. Could she also use this skillset to practice better self-care, for example, keeping a journal where she tracks and challenges her most stubborn self-narratives?

If you're seeking a simple set of guidelines that don't require you to compute too much, let's take a look at the following tips on simply taking action and getting into motion.

First, realize that almost every decision is reversible and you can backtrack to some degree. Therefore, it makes sense to dip your toe into one option to see what happens and gain some information, instead of standing at the fork in the road until you starve to death. You learn so much more by acting as if you are going to take one option instead of hemming and hawing about both. Only in the process of exploring an option will you learn more about it and how it feels.

If you are trying to decide between moving to New York or Texas, are you going to gain more information by visiting neither and continuing to debate with yourself, or by visiting one, seeing how you feel about it, and going through some motions to gain information? The point is that taking a few steps down one road is extremely reversible and worthwhile due to what you'll learn.

Second, as we discussed in an earlier chapter, apply strict boundaries to help make the choice for you. This streamlines your process and reduces the amount of thinking you have to do. For example, if you are struggling with what restaurant to pick for dinner, you might apply filters of healthy, inexpensive, within a ten-minute drive, and not hamburgers. After you set these boundaries, you might only have one or two choices left over. It's like when you shop online and apply filters for size, style, price, and color; suddenly you're left with only two shirts to buy.

If you're left with zero choices, remove one or two filters and work backward until you can make an easy yet satisfactory decision. You'll be left with choices that are within your criteria, and at that point, what does it matter? You can choose at random at this point with no loss in happiness or effectiveness, and you've successfully ignored everything that you *don't* care about.

A corollary to setting boundaries is to first decide upon a *default choice* if you can't decide within a set amount of time. Pick your default upfront, then set a time limit, where if you can't choose something else, you automatically go with the default. For instance, with your significant other, your default restaurant is an Italian joint. If you can't decide on a different restaurant within five minutes each night, then to Italy you go. This saves time, but the act of creating the default choice is also important because you will have automatically selected something that fits your requirements or desires. You'll be happy in either case, in other words.

In many instances, the default is what you had in mind the entire time and where you were probably going to end up regardless of any debate. You go through the mental exercise of choosing a "default" with the idea that you might end up there anyway.

Third, realize that you might have a drive to make the "perfect" decision. This is similar to our previous discussion about satisficing versus maximizing decisions, but it differs because perfection is the desire for something that doesn't exist.

If something checks all your boxes, that's all you need to beat your indecision. When you aim for perfection, you also tend to start running up against the law of diminishing returns, which states that the amount of effort you put into something isn't worth the return you gain anymore. For example, you might spend a hundred dollars on a pair of nice shoes. At that price point, they will be well-constructed, sturdy, and fashionable. What if you were to spend two hundred dollars on a similar pair of shoes? They'd still be well-constructed, sturdy, and fashionable.

This begs the question, were they worth the extra hundred bucks over the cheaper pair? For most people, no. There is a law of diminishing returns where the more expensive shoes don't make a difference in any relevant way. How nice can a pair of shoes get? Unless the more expensive shoes are self-cleaning with automatic lacing, you are spending more for essentially the same return.

You probably aren't shooting for life-changing restaurants every night of the week. In this case, your compulsion to make a perfect choice is wasted energy. Eating is the goal, not choosing a perfect meal. Unless you are making life-impacting choices that you will feel the repercussions of for years to come, attempting to make a perfect choice is silly. The difference between the "perfect" choice and the "good enough" choice will be negligible, and you might not even feel it, or remember it, the next day. There won't be consequences that make a difference in the long-term, so what is the sense in spending additional time and energy on it?

A famous comedian has clever input on this matter: "My rule is that if you have someone or something that gets seventy percent approval, you just do it, 'cause here's what happens. The fact that other options go away immediately brings your choice to eighty, because the pain of deciding is over."

Fourth, to make better and quicker decisions, engage in intentionally judgmental thinking. This is the type of thinking you have probably tried to repress, but it will be very beneficial for your decision-making. Think in black-and-white terms and reduce your decisions down to one to three main points.

Overgeneralize and don't look at the subtleties of your options. Willfully ignore the gray area and don't rationalize or justify statements by saying "But..." or "That's not *always* true..."

The idea is to focus on what really moves the needle for you and ignore elements that, while they matter, aren't the most important at the moment. Sometimes, consuming less information will help this because you are focused on a smaller set of factors.

Let's go back to the example of choosing a restaurant for dinner. How can you think more in black-and-white terms about something like this?

Simply reduce your restaurant choices down to what you might categorize as a first impression. Restaurant A is a place for burgers, despite the fact that five menu items are not burgers. It doesn't matter—in black-and-white terms, it's a burger place.

Restaurant B is expensive, despite the fact that it has five items that are cheap. It doesn't matter—in black-and-white terms, it's expensive. Restaurant C is far away, despite the fact that if you hit good traffic, it's not too far. It doesn't matter—in black-and-white terms, it is far.

Seeing options in black and white basically generalizes their traits and removes their subtleties. Remember, if we're talking about destroying indecision, this is one of the best things you can do. If you have a hazy stereotype of your two options and the stakes are relatively low, then that's all the information you need.

A final method to be intentionally judgmental is to sum up your options in one short sentence only, no commas or addendums allowed. You aren't allowed to elaborate on anything. When you try this, you'll notice you can only end up with broad strokes, such as "It's a burger place that's ten minutes away" versus "Well, they serve burgers, but they also have lasagna and tacos. It's ten minutes away, but I think we can get there faster." Which one is going to be easier for you to choose for or against?

The takeaway:

- Indecisiveness comes down to an intolerance of uncertainty, and often to informational overload. In our modern, technologically advanced world, we're constantly bombarded with an endless set of options in all spheres of life. We're also saturated with all the information we come across on a daily basis, and this makes it hard to decide on things because we're always looking for a better choice. We can consciously decide, however, to embrace imperfection and take on risks in the service of achieving what we care about.
- Another way to tackle information overload is to ascertain what you need to know in order to make a decision, and identify the outcome you're looking for. Then, narrow down possible decisions and take a leap of faith by choosing any because the opportunity cost involved becomes very low.

- Our fear of the unknown is something we have inherited from our ancestors because for most of human history, being suspicious of what we didn't know kept us alive and free from dangers. However, in the modern world, this fear can become catastrophic because we are constantly asked to make choices in areas where we have incomplete knowledge. In today's world, acting without knowing all the details is often necessary to avoid becoming paralyzed, and is unlikely to lead to the extreme danger it did in the distant past.
- We can become more decisive by applying the four steps of uncover, remove, reduce and transform. Critical thinking and data gathering are useful—if our target is healthy, and if it ultimately serves the end goal of conscious *action*. However, at some point we need to commit to taking an action. Think about whether a particular decision will take you closer to where you want to be, and if it does, go ahead with it.

- We can make better decisions when we slow down, turn inward to appraise our own values, and simplify our choices. We can also remember that it's OK to make mistakes—that's how we learn.

Chapter 4: The Block of Fixed Mindset

In a previous chapter, we saw that a self-defeating mental narrative can work against you, even and especially if it's in direct contravention of objective facts. Telling ourselves an inaccurate and unflattering story is one way we can block our ability to think intentionally, but we can also block ourselves when we entertain an entire attitude and way of being that negates growth, flexibility, change and learning.

This attitude can be summed up as a "fixed mindset." The concept of fixed mindset (and its healthier counterpart, a growth mindset) was first introduced by psychologist Carol Dweck, and goes a long way to describing the attitudinal orientation that lies behind many of our core beliefs.

For Dweck, success in life, your personality, behavior, identity, source of motivation and indeed your *entire lived experience*, comes down to whether you occupy a fixed or growth mindset when encountering other people, change or the unknown. Mindset matters—and it matters whether we are conscious of its influence or not.

A mindset is not a particular set of beliefs, statements or behaviors; rather, it is an approach to life. It's a *way* of being that determines how we see ourselves, our response to challenge and adversity, how we interpret events, how we construct our sense of self and meaning in the universe, our choice of goals and how we achieve them, and how we interact with others.

What is a fixed mindset? Essentially, it is the fundamental orientation that sees your nature (your intelligence, your skill, your personality, etc.) as fixed and innate, i.e. an inborn characteristic that is, well, fixed. This is the belief that your current qualities are unchangeable and static.

In other words:

We are born into this world with a set amount of intelligence that we can never change;
We have a fixed moral quality that makes us good or bad people, period;
We have our set personalities that will always stay what they are;
We are blessed with a certain complement of talents that we can never improve upon;

And so on. People who have a fixed mindset see life as a card game and their selfhood as a hand they're dealt. There are consequences to this worldview, however. If you have a fixed mindset, it affects *everything* you do and feel and think in life.

If you believe you aren't too bright, for example, you won't try all that hard to improve your intelligence, and you'll assume that other people's success occurs because they were simply born with a genius you weren't. With a fixed mindset, you'll never challenge yourself to be better than you are right now.

If you believe you're simply born a little lazy, or emotionally stunted, or are angry by nature, or simply have a preference for something that can never be questioned or changed, you conduct yourself accordingly: you never pursue any situations that would require you to rethink this assumption, or you actively seek out confirmation for this foregone conclusion about who you are. For instance, if you believe you're an angry person, you gravitate toward situations and relationships that will provoke you into displaying anger.

On the other hand, believing that intelligence is something you're born with and not something you work for, earn, or develop means you disempower yourself even if you happen to view yourself as quite smart. You still don't work to achieve your true potential, and downplay the value of hard work (and humility!). After all, if you didn't make an effort to achieve something, why would you value and appreciate it? Why take any pride and pleasure in it, if it's essentially a random mistake?

The trouble with a fixed mindset is how it leads you to respond to challenges—which are nothing less than precious invitations to grow and learn. If you believe you simply can't learn, and that nothing can substantially change for you, you will shy away from challenge. After all, doing things that are difficult, uncertain or uncomfortable just sounds like subjecting yourself to a hassle for no benefit. Why bother when you can't really improve who you are?

A fixed mindset has a sneaky way of becoming real. When you shirk away from challenge, avoid discomfort, downplay genuine effort and hard work, give up easily or discount the success of others, you only limit yourself and essentially create the reality in which you are as small as you believe you are. Thoughts, again, create your experience.

In addition, with a fixed mindset, the ego enters more easily into the picture. This is because traits, when they are viewed as fixed, are felt to be more a part of the ego than they probably are. We don't see our intelligence or creativity or kindness as something we *do*, but rather as someone we *are*—and this sense of attachment can naturally lead us to feel quite defensive.

We can get carried away with trying to prove things to ourselves or others, to bluff that we know more than we do. We fail to admit when we don't know something, and so we never learn. We might pretend that we already understand everything (and forego the chance to genuinely learn about it) rather than be seen as ignorant. This is because if we have a fixed mindset, then being wrong means we will *always* be wrong. Appearing stupid for a few seconds means we *are* stupid, permanently, and in a way that can never change.

We saw this dynamic in our example of the employee who messed up at work. We saw that his conception of himself was as a genius overachiever, who was supremely competent. We can infer that this was the foundation of his identity and self-worth—not something he merely did, but something he *was*.

Making a mistake challenged this identity, and this felt so uncomfortable that the employee would rather avoid it completely: deny it, run away, or blame someone else. Why wouldn't he? The alternative was to conclude that he *wasn't* a genius after all, and therefore was a (permanently) bad and disappointing person who had no hope of being anything else.

Can you see how this mindset, ironically, almost guarantees people will experience precisely the thing they fear?

When we encounter the unknown, it's a chance to expand understanding. When we come across something we don't comprehend or lack mastery over, it's a chance to learn. When we experience our own limitations, it's a chance to grow.

If we're determined to see ourselves as already all-knowing, already grown, already in full understanding (i.e. "fixed"), we shut ourselves off from every possible process of self-development and improvement. This is obvious, when you think about it: we can never learn the answer unless we are willing to admit we don't currently know it. We cannot grow and improve unless we are courageous and honest enough to admit that we could stand to grow and become better than we are, right now.

Things that are fixed, don't grow. They don't learn, either.

Enter the growth mindset. This is the worldview and corresponding attitude that sees life as in progress, and your essential character as something that is somewhat malleable and up for change. In other words, the growth mindset acknowledges that although we are born with some fixed characteristics, a lot of who we are comes down to what we *do*—and that can change.

This is the belief that whatever we are now, we can learn to be different.

We can change. We can improve. Whether we succeed in life comes down to the actions we take, the (intentional) effort and hard work. Sure, some people may be born with more talent, privilege or raw luck. But when it comes to our lives, we are conscious agents who can determine the quality of our being because we can work hard, act with consciousness and make choices.

Sound familiar? The growth mindset is more or less the same as what we mean by "intentional thinking." Rather than passively, unconsciously accepting that we are as we are and that's that, we take conscious and willful control of the course of our lives.

The attitude translates into real success. This is because when we encounter obstacles, we don't shrug and give up—we understand that we can overcome them if we work harder. We're not humiliated and discouraged when we don't understand something, when we make a mistake or when we come up against something difficult. We don't take this to mean that we are, at our core, bad people. We simply accept it as par for the course and get on with the hard work!

With a growth mindset, we don't see adversity as a problem at all—why would we, when it doesn't say anything about our natures, our identities, or our value as people? We embrace discomfort and confusion because we know they are signs that we are learning... and we want to learn! We accept criticism without being defensive. We have nothing to prove. Our only mission is to get better, and we do this by accepting our faults and misunderstandings as quickly as possible.

To return to the question of comparison with others, when we adopt a growth mindset, we become less threatened by the success of other people around us. We needn't be threatened, and don't say bitterly "well, lucky them, they were just born that way." Instead, we can celebrate other people's success with them, and be inspired to know that if we work hard, we too can improve. We don't dwell in the disempowered state of mind tells us that we could never have what others have—instead, we ask *how* we can.

In this mindset, it's OK to be a beginner. In fact, it's a prerequisite on any journey of improvement! It's acceptable to find things difficult. Struggling with a life goal doesn't mean we weren't cut out for it and that we should give up and leave it for people who it comes "naturally" to; it only means we are doing something difficult, and that takes effort.

This is a mindset that runs deep. Ask yourself, where does success *really* come from? Who are you, as a person, and what are your limitations, your possibilities?

Maybe you've quietly resigned yourself to a situation because you unconsciously don't believe it's possible or worth it to try for something different. Maybe you've been assuming that living your best life was supposed to feel less like hard work, and so you've given up on your dreams prematurely.

Maybe you've deliberately kept yourself from learning and growing because you're more concerned with *appearing* to already have everything together—and isn't that a shame?

With a growth mindset, failure never defines you. Your experience is always in process, always up to you to classify, to own. A mistake is simply something you do. It's not a judgment against your character. You can hold on to it in shame, or you can learn your lesson and move on to what's really important: becoming what you really want to become.

With a growth mindset, you don't avoid discomfort—in fact, you may seek it out. After all, it's this slightly uncomfortable place just outside your comfort zone where all the magic happens… so why would you avoid it when it's literally the place where your dreams come true? It's the difference between "I can't do this" and "I can't do this… yet." One stunts you and keeps you stuck where you are. The other opens you up to hopeful possibilities, to the energy of problem-solving, to creative next steps.

It's tricky to spot a fixed mindset in action, but most of us, being raised in the cultures and educational systems we have, suffer from this mindset to some degree. How often do we praise a successful person for being a "genius" versus acknowledging that they're just like us, only they worked damn hard? How often do we feel like making one mistake proves that we are complete, irremediable idiots?

We return to the big idea running through this entire book: that our thoughts create our experience. Our mindset determines our thoughts, feelings and, ultimately, our actions, which then shape our world, creating feedback loops that confirm and reinforce whatever ideas we have programmed into these powerful machines called our minds.

There's nothing all that magical about a growth mindset. It's merely a subtle shift in perspective—looking at exactly the same thing as everyone else, but seeing something a little different. So, just as in our example of the employee above, adversity and failure are always there, only our interpretation changes. One way is to see failure as a condemnation; the other is to embrace it as a gift, a teacher, an inspiring challenge.

Any time you say something like, "I'm just not someone who's good at budgeting" or decide not to try something new because you're afraid of looking silly, a fixed mindset stands between you and the full potential of a more empowered, intentional way of being.

The Gift of Failing

We all will fail. That's a given.

When we come into this world, we know how to do very, very little, and we understand even less. As infants, we are utterly helpless. But we are also little bundles of *potential*.

When we learn to do anything—walk, talk, eat with a spoon—we have to move from a position of ignorance and incompetence to one of understanding and ability. We can never, never move instantly from one state to the other; it always takes time, a little trial and error, and a lot of "failure."

Failure is what success looks like in process. Failure is the mechanism of learning.

Failure is not really failure at all; it's simply a natural, valuable part of the process of acquiring skills, understanding and wisdom. There is no way around it—every adult was once an infant who fell on their butts again and again as they struggled to master the art of walking. Every one of us has failed millions of times already, in the service of becoming who we are today.

Thankfully for us, babies have no shame. They're learning machines and have not been indoctrinated into being embarrassed about the path they need to take to figure things out. They just do it. Later, as we grow up, we learn another lesson: that struggle, effort, confusion or mistakes are wrong, and make us bad people. Isn't it ironic, though? All of us want to be intelligent and accomplished, but we are all squeamish when it comes to the very process that would take us there: so-called "failure"!

When you apply your conscious, intentional will to the inevitability of failure, you give yourself the opportunity to interpret and frame the experience according to your own values. *You get to redeem failure, by transforming it into an opportunity to learn.*

There are loads of benefits to failure! Failing teaches you, primarily, to be better. Aren't you so lucky to have a kindly, wise old master called life, who is always ready and willing to show you where you need to improve? Failure teaches you to let go of your ego. More often than not, ego will only hold you back, inhibit your power to evolve and grow, and make life's ordinary slips and hurdles more painful than they need to be.

Failure teaches you to be humble. To stay on your toes and never get too comfy with one level of mastery—there is always another horizon, and we are always beginners. Failure makes us more keenly appreciate mastery when we do achieve it, because we understand its price. Could we have felt as honored to be smart or rich or wise if we were simply given it all for free?

Failure is character building—if we engage it honestly and with conscious intention. The next time you fail, pause and try to become aware of yourself in that very moment. Look at your thoughts and emotions.

- Notice any stories you're compelled to tell yourself ("See? You've failed again, you knew this was a bad idea..." or "people are going to be so disappointed in you...")
- Choose to set these stories aside for a moment and remind yourself

that failure is something you do, not something you are.
- Turn your attention to what can be done from this point on. How can you use this failure to fuel and energize the next step? What can you do better next time? Commit to taking even a small step in that direction, right now.

By following the three steps above, you may notice that you eventually learn to take the ego sting out of not getting things 100 percent right. Consciously choosing beneficial action is incredibly empowering. It reminds you of who's really in control: you. It brings your focus right back to what you are really in control of: yourself.

In time, you may start to understand how silly it is to fear failure. You'll see that you're still who you are, still a worthy and valuable person even if you mess up here and there, or don't know how to do something right the first time around. You may even start inviting mistakes—after all, they provide valuable data. Every "no" is actually one step closer to the "yes" you want, if you think like a scientist and see your failure as merely feedback on the hypothesis you're posing.

If you mess up, have a sense of humor about it. Own up to any poor behavior, take full responsibility, and feel how this instantly gives you back your power and invites you to move on to the next step: try again. Trying to master something difficult and needing countless attempts to get it right is not a mistake or a failure at all. It's simply the cost of your learning. Smile at every step in this process and trust that with an open, growth-oriented mindset, you're getting closer to where you want to be.

"How you do anything is how you do everything"—you don't need to focus so intently on specific individual actions if you have a robust, healthy growth mindset informing all your decisions and powering your core beliefs. And perhaps more than anything else, a growth mindset can radically and authentically transform all your limiting beliefs.

This all ties in very neatly with the four steps we outlined in the first chapter: **uncover, remove, reduce and transform.**

Let's say with some reflection and self-inquiry, you discover that you have some beliefs that typify a fixed mindset. You begin by trying to **uncover** the root cause of this mindset. Maybe you notice that you say things like, "Well, it's easy for her to lose weight, she has good genes, but I guess I was just designed to be fat," and "Well, I'm just the sort of person that really loves food!"

These beliefs can come from a range of different places. Perhaps you have friends and family who express similar sentiments. Perhaps your culture or society taught you this. Perhaps the billion-dollar weight-loss industry has gotten into your head, convincing you that losing weight is ultra-complicated, and basically impossible unless you have some esoteric knowledge you paid for, or a special supplement or crazy diet on your side.

Once you've identified these thoughts and attitudes, you bring a little consciousness into things, noticing yourself thinking them when you do. Slowly, you can work to **remove** them. You can deliberately replace the above thoughts with a more realistic and active one, for example, "I have the choice to improve my health, right now. I can lose weight with effort."

Though in some sense this is a more difficult position to take, on the other hand it is more empowering to take responsibility for your own well-being—because once you do, you suddenly hold your own success in your hands, even if it is difficult to do so. To cultivate this sense of empowerment, you can take action. Even small steps point in the right direction.

If you truly do doubt your ability to lose weight, you can start by establishing a small daily habit that will help, for example simply eating 100 calories less a day. In a few months, you will notice weight loss. This can be encouraging and reinforce the healthier, more growth-mindset position: that you can control your weight. In fact, you are the *only one* who can.

You can certainly **reduce** your fixed mindset, but there's no need to eliminate it entirely. It's reasonable, for example, to acknowledge the fact that you probably won't lose half your body weight in two months, no matter how strong your willpower. By reducing this mental block, you can still retain some of the benefits of realizing that a few things are truly out of your control. You cannot significantly change your body shape, your height, or your age, for example. But we can still acknowledge all this with conscious acceptance, taking responsibility for the things we can.

Finally, you can **transform** your fixed mindset into something that really works for you. It may sound strange, but why not take the fatalism and resignation that comes with a fixed mindset and apply it to a new fact: that you are 100 percent in control and responsible for your life. There is nothing you can do about this fact. You *are* born with a certain fixed nature or quality—the quality of being completely, constantly changing and growing!

Let's take some of these insights and apply them to real-life, practical situations. What does it actually look like to have a growth mindset?

1. Accept your flaws joyfully and with a sense of humor. Own all your weaknesses; they're not impediments to success, but the very raw material you will use to cultivate personal development. Be honest and forthright about your bad sides. Laugh at your mistakes—it's not really such a big deal to be imperfect!
2. Put learning, understanding and growth as a priority over other people's opinions and judgments. Approval just isn't as important. Making gradual, consistent improvements is far, far more valuable.
3. Focus on process rather than outcome. Set goals by all means, but focus on what you actually control every day: habits. Commit to small, repeatable actions. Praise and reward yourself for the right attitude, and for consistency, rather than for what you actually achieve. Always challenge yourself—if you're not a little uncomfortable, keep pushing until you are!

The takeaway:

- A fixed mindset is one where you believe that all of your qualities such as intelligence, motivation levels, your skills, and so on, are all inherently a part of you in pre-decided quantities that cannot ever be changed. This mindset precludes growth and the cultivation of our conscious intention; it tells us that any effort to improve is ultimately meaningless, because you can never be better than you already are.
- Instead, we can adopt a growth mindset and engage our conscious will to choose the self and the life we want, rather than passively accept the status quo. We tell ourselves that with the right amount of effort and the correct approach, we can be the person we want to be. If we aren't good at something, enough practice will help us improve and eventually master that activity.
- With a growth mindset, we see failure as the gift it is: an opportunity to learn and prove that we are evolving and changing. Fixed

mindsets teach us that failures are something to be scared of, and to avoid because they are a damning indictment of us as individuals. We view them as judgments rather than as merely part of the process of learning. However, growth mindsets help us see failures in a positive light because they represent the potential to be better.
- We can develop a growth mindset by abandoning grand goals somewhere off in the distance and instead focus on tiny, consistent daily habits that bring us closer and closer to excellence. Having a growth mindset involves valuing the process over the outcome, letting go of outlandish expectations for ourselves, accepting our shortcomings, and prioritizing learning to improve above all else.

Chapter 5: The Block of Self-Deception

As you read through the previous chapters, you probably noticed something with many of the given examples. The starting step for any process of improvement always seems to be "gain conscious awareness," and yet, this is much easier said than done.

Imagine a person who goes to therapy to get a handle on their depression and anxiety. Once there, the therapist helps explore the possible causes and triggers behind some of their client's thoughts, feelings and behaviors. But rather than honestly appraising issues like addiction, trauma, poor choices in the past, childhood experiences or bad health habits, the client simply decides that the real problem is that everyone is jealous of them.

The impulse to seek personal development is there (hence going to therapy), but something has gone wrong: self-deception. Maybe the person in our example does something else like claim that literally 100 percent of the problems in their life are because of their awful partner, or refuse to acknowledge a painful truth that would in the long run help them heal.

The weakness in many of the previous chapters' examples is that they rely on us being honest with ourselves. Here, we see the same themes revisited—can we tolerate discomfort, "failure," uncertainty, criticism? Can we claim responsibility for ourselves and take ownership of our lives, even if it's a little scary or feels a lot like hard work? This is the difference between a passive, reactive and fixed mindset, and a conscious, deliberate and proactive one that sets you up to take charge of your life.

Now, there isn't any value judgment in any of this. *All* of us can practice self-deception and be a little deluded at times. There's a reason for it: doing so protects us from uncomfortable truths. Self-comforting can go too far, and we can find ourselves telling convenient little lies that ultimately limit us. It's only human, but that doesn't mean we can't do something about it.

Overcoming this mental block requires a lot of courage—both to honestly identify where it's happening in the first place, and also to willfully abandon any comfortable illusions in favor of a likely less comfortable truth. Living in a world of your own deceptions does have some perks! But as we'll see in this chapter, the costs may actually be more than they're worth, and it's a real understanding of this fact that can allow you to gradually loosen self-deception and intentionally cultivate more resilience and honesty.

The trouble with self-delusion is obvious: it's almost impossible to spot, by design.

It's a tricky problem. How can you ever really know if you're lying to yourself? What a rabbit hole to fall into: the question of what's really the "truth" and what is an unacceptably inaccurate interpretation. After all, isn't the claim in this book that our thoughts determine our experience? Aren't we deliberately trying to cultivate, in a way, certain positive illusions in ourselves?

In fact, overcoming self-delusion is not nearly as complicated as all this. It all comes down, again, to the stories we tell ourselves, our value judgments, and our expectations. If we follow the *emotion*, we will soon arrive at any less-than-accurate white lies we are holding on to.

How to Identify Self-Delusion

1. Have self-compassion. Remember, self-delusion is there to serve a purpose—to shield you from painful truths. You can only peek at these painful truths if you're genuinely willing to believe that "whatever truth I uncover about myself, I accept with kindness." Try not to judge yourself or feel shame. Just become curious and remember, you're not trying to attack yourself. Self-understanding is about loving yourself enough to change with kindness.

2. Next, zoom in on your defense mechanisms. You'll know you're employing a defense mechanism when you feel defensive, or suddenly and irrationally emotional about something. These "buttons" are a clue that there is hidden and unacknowledged material in your psyche. Proceed gently, instead of avoiding or denying. For example, if you've always been touchy about your weight (like the woman in our previous example) and one day feel criticized, stay with the angry feelings that may emerge. Could it be that the person "criticizing" you has said something a little close to home? Unravel this thread to find where you may be telling yourself little white lies.

3. Look out for absolute language, i.e. words like "always," "never," "completely." Watch for black-and-white thinking, i.e. something is all one thing or all another, without any gray area in between. This signals an inability to tolerate nuance, i.e. reality! Look at the stories you tell. The self-deluded ones may be overly

simplistic, primarily emotional in content and have an absolute quality about them (for example, it's the difference between "I can't help it, I have fat genes, I'll always be a fat ass" and "Man, losing weight is hard!")

4. Self-delusion often goes along with a failure to take responsibility. Psychologists talk about your locus of control, i.e. where you see agency arising from. Grounded, realistic thinking acknowledges external factors but largely works from an internal locus of control—that is, it takes personal responsibility and ownership of what happens in life. Self-delusion in contrast may have the flavor of blame, passivity, and victimhood.

5. Sometimes, a self-delusional mental story is one that is convoluted. Have you noticed how people telling a lie will often go on and on, adding countless unnecessary details, i.e. "protesting too much"? When we lie to ourselves, we sometimes do the same. The truth doesn't need lengthy excuses and justifications; it can often be stated quickly. If you find

yourself getting carried away in what you think is a reason, pause and ask if it's actually an excuse.

As you can see, this isn't easy work, and it's not something you do in an afternoon and tick off the list forever. Combating self-delusion is hard, because we are the only ones who will ever really hold ourselves accountable. We can lie effectively to others, and to ourselves, and never be challenged to be better. *We* have to ask more of ourselves.

Is it really true that you could have completed an MBA, only you chose not to because you thought it would be too easy? Is it really true that the only reason you're single is because you're too nice? Is it really true that you drink so much because your job requires it?

Sometimes, we delude ourselves with a story of what we think *should* be the case. It can be helpful to look more closely at this "should" narrative and ask where it came from, whether it's true, and if you really like the way it makes you feel, think and behave.

Overly high expectations can cause us to believe we need to be perfect, need to be happy all the time, need to be in complete control (are you seeing echoes of the fixed mindset here?). We may have succumbed to external ideas of what we need to be—smart, wealthy, attractive, happy etc.—and constructed little white lies to cover the difference between those lofty ideals and how we *really* feel.

But, with a growth mindset, an attitude of deliberate and conscious intention, and bucketloads of self-compassion, we see that it's not the end of the world to be what we are. Even if we're sometimes confused, broke, sad, or unappealing to others. In fact, if we hope to change reality, we need to be able to look at it honestly first, without any distortions.

It may not always feel like it, but integrity and resilience are actually the more valuable traits to develop. We don't dwell on our flaws because we're masochistic or hate ourselves—we do it because we value growth.

We value ourselves and our experience. Yes, it may be tempting, for example, to always be the victim and blame someone else for our problems. But the more conscious view sees that this position isn't all that satisfying, because it never empowers you to make meaningful changes, never encourages you to own your own agency. Isn't there more to life than comfort?

A Look at Defense Mechanisms

Essentially, a defense mechanism exists for one purpose: to protect your ego. They're like a wall you build between yourself and any unpleasant emotions, thoughts or memories you don't feel able to cope with. Any unwanted feeling can trigger a defense mechanism, but the process is almost always unconscious.

The goal is not to completely rid yourself of defense mechanisms—it's healthy and normal to have an ego that you want to protect, and we all need a bit of a cushion between us and the sometimes harsh realities around us!

The trick is to become *aware* of what we're doing and why. With awareness comes choice, and the possibility of doing something different. Something better. Awareness puts you in control, rather than having you merely be at the mercy of unconscious forces.

You don't need to get carried away with psychoanalyzing yourself; even becoming aware of just the tip of the iceberg means you can start to hold yourself accountable and find healthier ways of coping with unpleasant emotions, even using them to inspire growth and development.

The most common and basic defense mechanism is plain old **denial**. You simply refuse to see the facts staring you right in the face. When faced with extremely distressing situations that we might struggle to cope with, our brains respond by simply shutting themselves off to the truth in order to avoid a confrontation between our internal perception and reality. For example: Despite being confronted with ample evidence that they are seriously ill and will die soon, a person may refuse to think about it and avoid the topic entirely.

Another example is believing that you're "just a social drinker" when in reality you have a serious drinking problem. Nobody wants to view themselves as an addict, and so they just refuse to believe anything that might indicate as much. If you suspect that you're in denial about something in your life, consider whether you tend to avoid thinking about that fact or avoid situations which may make you question your perception of things. If you do, you might be utilizing this defense mechanism.

Projection is another common one, and it happens whenever we take rejected parts of our own psyche and attribute them to others. The common story of the rabidly homophobic minister secretly being gay themselves is an example, as is the tendency people have to suspect others purely because they themselves are behaving suspiciously.

If you tend to project your emotions onto others frequently, that might be an indication of you not knowing yourself well enough. This is because projection often results from an inability to accept our own thoughts and emotions, and so we attribute them to others in order to avoid feeling bad about ourselves. Those who have low self-esteem or suffer from an inferiority complex are also prone to using projection. By working on these underlying issues, you'll recognize yourself using projection as a defense mechanism much more easily.

A slightly different coping mechanism is **displacement**, where we take our emotions and express them toward a more acceptable target, instead of where they really belong—for example, blaming your bad mood on the daily commute when you're really unhappy in your job.
While displacement may allow you to express your emotions toward less risky targets, it prevents you from learning how to appropriately deal with them. It can also result in you hurting people who are completely innocent, and these are generally the people you love most. If you find yourself constantly taking out your frustrations on particular people because you feel that it is "safe" to do so, you may be overusing this defense mechanism.

Repression occurs when we push unwanted emotions out of awareness, a little like denial but much harder to resolve. The difference between the two is that repression involves a complete burial of painful memories or experiences deep in your subconscious, whereas the thing you're in denial about is still in the realm of your conscious awareness.

Difficult thoughts or bad memories can still haunt our dreams or unconsciously guide our behavior. Repression is arguably the most difficult defense mechanism to identify. However, some useful indicators are having nightmares with repetitive themes, angry outbursts or disproportionate levels of anxiety due to certain triggers, etc.

Regression is less common, but makes a lot of sense—we regress (escape) to an earlier developmental stage when we feel threatened or overwhelmed. This is common in children (for example, beginning to suck your thumb again after a trauma) but also occurs in adults. Have you ever seen a grown-up throw a "tantrum"?

They may have been using this coping mechanism.

Defense mechanisms are seldom this simple, though. The most persistent and difficult ones are the hardest to spot. **Rationalization** is a tricky one, especially when employed by intelligent people. It means we use "facts" to justify and explain what are really irrational, emotional impulses.

So if you stood a friend up because they're usually late for your meetings, you've rationalized away bad behavior on your part. One trick to identify rationalization is to try and put yourself in the spot of a third person who has been offered the justification you just gave yourself. You'll likely see the flaw in your reasoning.

Intellectualization is related, where we distance ourselves from our emotions by engaging fully in cold, hard facts—sadly an impulse that is sometimes rewarded in our culture!

There are many other defense mechanisms, but you get the idea. However many painful, difficult emotions exist, there are as many ways to avoid, deny or minimize our experience of them. What's important is not the many different ways we can deceive ourselves, but rather how we can step outside of this self-deception and toward conscious, intentional thinking instead.

Becoming aware of your psychological "blind spots" requires a little bravery, and a willingness to be honest with yourself. If you have friends and family you really trust, you might be surprised at their answers if you ask them to help you recognize your defense mechanisms in action. After all, these defenses often appear in our relationships with others, so these people may have keen insights into things you yourself are unaware of.

A therapist can play the same role, with the added benefit of offering an anonymous space where you don't feel judged. Remember that defense mechanisms serve a purpose—try not to get rid of them without ensuring that you can replace them with other, healthier coping strategies.

This is where we return to our four-step process, which is not just about removing harmful mental blocks, but also about replacing them with something better. Defense mechanisms can seem pretty scary, but they are nothing more than beliefs. And beliefs can be changed.

Let's consider a very common scenario, and one that you're likely to identify with in some shape or form. Consider a woman who feels bad about herself. Imagine she hates the way she looks, and feels ashamed about many of her life decisions. Let's say she married someone she now realizes is a terrible match for her, had a child she didn't really want, and works at a job she doesn't actually enjoy.

These are pretty heavy truths. Acknowledging them head-on would be incredibly painful and disruptive; what's more, they'd demand that the woman change. And that's scary. She'd have to get divorced, or change jobs. And what about her child? What on earth could be done about those feelings?

The woman protects herself from this disruptive, painful information. She refused to acknowledge it's there at all (denial) and may even go over the top trying to convince herself and others that the opposite is true, by doting on her children and loudly claiming how in love with her husband she is (this is a defense mechanism called reaction formation, by the way).

She could also work hard to repress these ugly feelings, but they may come out in dreams or slips of the tongue. She may even unconsciously sabotage her marriage or make "mistakes" at work that could get her fired. Through it all she could engage with rationalization and justification, telling herself convoluted stories that cleverly conceal her true feelings even from herself.

Perhaps most interestingly, she may end up projecting—this is the super-dedicated mom who is full of judgment for other women. She finds herself being mean to women who don't have children, calling them selfish. She scoffs at other people's relationships and believes that everyone is secretly unhappy but pretending otherwise. When someone around her appears to have made a mistake, she heaps on the scorn and judgment (that would ordinarily have been directed toward herself) and spares herself the truth.

The defense mechanisms are doing their job—the woman remains completely unaware of her real feelings, having pinned them all on someone else, and her ego is saved the upsetting disruption that being honest would bring. This is a dynamic that you will see play out not just individually, but with families, communities, even entire nations.

It's a common political adage that if you want to know what your own country's government is doing in secret, look at what they loudly declare their enemies to be doing. The same principle of denial and projection is underway. "They are terrorists but *we* are brave freedom fighters" is nothing more than a rationalization.

No matter how big and stubborn the defense mechanism, however, it can be removed with patience, honesty, bravery, self-compassion and a commitment to living with conscious intention and integrity.

The woman in our example can **uncover** the reasons for her defense mechanisms by asking *why* she feels and thinks as she does. There are several layers to this: Why does she feel that her life choices were a mistake? But why also does she feel that having made these mistakes is so unforgivable?

By looking closely at her core beliefs and narratives, she can become more aware of them as they occur, gradually bringing this material into consciousness. She can start to **remove** them, deliberately replacing them with thoughts such as, "I can't change the past, but I can choose my behavior right now," or "I am not a bad person if I make a mistake."

Of course, bearing in mind that we don't want to completely eradicate defense mechanisms, only **reduce** them, she can adopt a moderate, understanding attitude toward herself. Though it's true that she can learn to forgive herself for making choices that were wrong for her, she can also use her life experience as a lesson, teaching herself never to compromise on what she really wants, and to take full and conscious ownership for her one and only precious life. It's this attitude that will bring her closest to a life that she actually does desire.

In this way, her difficult emotions and her defense mechanisms can be transformed into something valuable, and an opportunity to grow and be better. It won't be easy. It certainly won't be pleasant. But it will be honest and brave, and it will be the single best chance she has of living a life of honesty, integrity and purpose.

Growth and comfort: two mutually exclusive values

This leads us to the nub of what we can learn from tackling this particular mental block. Defense mechanisms and all other kinds of self-delusion are basically different ways for us to ensure our comfort and security. They keep us in the status quo, nice and cozy, where nothing ever changes.

As useful as they are at this job, defense mechanisms simultaneously keep us away from change, growth, development, learning, understanding and insight. To put it bluntly, they keep us from *living*.

Here's the truth: self-deception feels good. It's convenient, it doesn't challenge us and it's nice and comfortable. Many of us get trapped in self-deception simply because it offers such a comforting alternative to reality! Another truth is that sometimes, we are *forced* out of our comfort zones rather than electing to leave them of our own accord. In other words, our self-deception no longer holds, or an external disruption compels us to look honestly at things we'd rather not.

When the pain of staying as you are is greater than the pain of changing, you'll change. When the rewards of developing and growing are greater than the rewards of staying just as you are, you'll take the leap. But wouldn't it be great if you consciously stepped outside of your own comfort zone *before* it got to this point?

Self-deception may feel good, but we need to be honest with ourselves: *growth and comfort are mutually exclusive.* We can grow and develop and achieve all the goals we want to for ourselves, or we can stay nice and safe and comfortable. But we can't do both at the same time.

The price of comfort is stagnation. It's deliberately leaving some potential on the table, unfulfilled. It's the easy way out.

The price of striving for your dreams, however, is hard work. It's the effort required to face your fears, and to keep going even when you're lazy or unsure or scared. It's the hard way—but it's so, so much more rewarding.

When you prioritize safety and comfort, you're playing to *not lose* the game of life. You are hedging your bets, playing small, avoiding risk and challenge, and shying away from the tough questions. But in trying to avoid negativity, the cruel irony is that we also end up avoiding all the positivity that comes with it: the satisfaction of achievement, the pride at building something, at facing fears, growing in wisdom and courage.

When we prioritize growth, we are playing *to win*. It's an entirely different attitude.

This is a positive, proactive, conscious and purpose-driven approach to a life that has the courage to intentionally pursue or create what is important.

Life is a package deal: the rough always comes with the smooth. When our strategy is to avoid bad emotion, we actually end up avoiding *all* emotion, good and bad. To shut ourselves off from pain is to shut ourselves off from life itself, from learning opportunities, from the gift of "failing," improving, experiencing, living. There is no easy, comfortable life—this is an illusion.

So, what is the solution? Cold, unflinching honesty 100 percent of the time? Relentlessly pursuing big-ticket goals, no matter if it nearly kills you to do so?

Balance is key. And the only way to achieve balance is to turn up to the task of creating your life with deliberate, conscious intention and a commitment to honesty. Decide that you will not let unconscious forces direct and control your life—that job is reserved for your aware, purpose-driven self.

Consciously embrace your vulnerabilities

You can hold yourself accountable while still being kind to yourself. You can be honest but still understanding. You can seek to be somewhere better while still appreciating where you are right now, and all you've been through to get there. It's simple. Here's a practical method you can try right now.

First, as always, become aware. Ask, *"Where am I right now?"*

Look at your life, your situation, the facts around you, both general and specific. Notice if you're blaming others (your horrible parents, your boss, the government, God himself...) or complaining passively. Observe what behaviors you are defaulting to. Notice the stories you're telling yourself, and the emotional core behind those stories.

Next, ask yourself, with as much compassion as you can muster, *"How is this working for me?"* Become curious about the results you're achieving by thinking/believing/behaving in the ways you've identified. If you noticed a defense mechanism at work, ask honestly, even if it *is* keeping you "safe," is it bringing you any closer to being the kind of person you want to be?

The final question naturally follows: given that you've identified a way of being that simply isn't congruent with your values or the goals you want to achieve, ask, *"How can I change, right now?"* What actions would you like to take instead, acknowledging that this path may well be more challenging?

You don't have to make quantum leaps. In fact, you can make significant changes by simply asking what small thing you can do right now, that moves you closer to what matters, and away from an unconscious, passive, fearful frame of mind.

The women in our example can start small: by admitting *to herself* how she really feels, and deciding that she will no longer lie to herself, nor judge herself for what's already happened in the past. She can make a promise to herself to stop criticizing and judging other women; instead, when she notices this impulse, she can turn inward and remind herself that it's OK to make a mistake, and that she is always able to choose purpose-driven action instead.

The takeaway:

- Self-delusion is the biggest mental block to our full and honest awareness. All of us delude ourselves about reality to some extent; it is nothing to be ashamed of. However, self-deception has many negative consequences for our growth as individuals, and we must identify what it is about our lives that we have chosen to blind ourselves to, in order to avoid ignoring opportunities to work on our flaws.
- We know self-delusion is at play if we recognize defense mechanisms, which develop to protect our ego from uncomfortable truths. Nobody can tackle our defense mechanisms but us. There are many common mechanisms such as denial, repression, regression, projection, displacement, etc. Each can be identified through its own unique

indicators, but the thing unifying them all is that they allow us to stay in a comfortable bubble where we can get away with not challenging ourselves enough to experience substantial growth.
- To live with more integrity and honesty, we need to acknowledge that growth and comfort are mutually exclusive. Can we accept *all* that we are, even the dark and unwanted parts of ourselves? We must, because that is the only way we can ever improve. Pain, failure, mistakes; all of these are a part of life and we must not run away from them, because life is a package deal. The good life is never lived in a state of comfort devoid of hardships.
- When we can embrace our vulnerabilities with honesty and self-compassion, we can empower ourselves to act with more focused intention—and live the life we want.

Chapter 6: The Block of Discomfort

So far, the blocks we've considered have assumed that there is some (often unconscious) psychological mechanism behind our inability to act with our full will and intention. But what if… you're just lazy?

"The block of discomfort" should actually be called "the block of the inability to tolerate discomfort," which most people simply label laziness. "Lazy" is a pretty loaded word, and has some heavy moral implications. It seems to suggest some inbuilt trait or characteristic that prevents people from striving adequately toward their own self-identified goals.

For the purposes of this book, however, we're going to assume that there's actually no such thing as laziness. People act against their own interests for many reasons. Fear, low self-esteem, social conditioning, habit, confusion or genuine exhaustion can all cause us to procrastinate, to hold back, to delay acting. But being "lazy" is not a cause so much as an effect. It's a symptom of a deeper problem: an unfocused, undisciplined will.

If your conscious intention is a muscle, laziness is like being out of shape. It's not that you absolutely *can't* lift that heavy weight; it's more like your muscles are simply not conditioned enough to do so. With time, practice and diligent effort, you become stronger and it becomes easier to do what you need to do.

When we continually fail to use our conscious intention, it becomes slack and underdeveloped in exactly the same way. We need to consistently *push* to strengthen it—in the same way that muscles need to work hard, to resist gravity, to push and pull, your willpower needs to push up against adversity, challenge and difficulty. In other words, discomfort.

Laziness is not some personality trait or moral judgment. It's simply a state of being untrained. This is not something to be ashamed of or discouraged by, in the same way as it's not bad to be a newbie when it comes to strength training and fitness.

The problem is the story we tell about discomfort, about what it means, and our willingness to endure it. In other words, it's all about our belief. To keep the exercise analogy going, imagine a person who wants to train for a marathon, from scratch. On the first day of training, they notice a slight stitch in their side and feel a little muscle soreness the next morning. Wouldn't it be ridiculous if they concluded that running just wasn't for them and they might as well quit and never try again?

And yet so many of us do the same when it comes to more abstract goals. We assume that discomfort, difficulty, even outright pain and hardship means something is wrong. That we're on the wrong path, or that if we find it hard now we will always find it hard, and so what's the point?

Perhaps we can blame the once-popular "follow your bliss" school of thought that seemed to suggest that if you just seek your dreams and listen to your heart, life will be easy and harmonious and flow without a single snag, and you'll never again have to suffer the humiliation of being an awkward, fumbling beginner.

Sounds nice, but the result of this belief is that you quit the very second you experience a little hurdle in the path. Even worse, you gravitate to only those tasks in life that are likely to challenge you the least—the path of least resistance. It doesn't take a genius to see that this mindset, though comforting in the short-term, is a one-way ticket to mediocrity.

In essence, it's not really our innate ability to tolerate discomfort that's at stake here, but rather our *belief* about that ability. Have you ever met a person who almost seemed offended that life didn't cater perfectly to their every whim? Someone who felt entitled to have things go easily for them? Perhaps you yourself are that person. In our industrialized, materialistic society, we can start to see ourselves as consumers rather than creators, always asking what we get out of the deal long before we've considered what we're willing to put in.

Self-discipline can seem unfashionable for some, especially those who would prefer that positive thinking alone be enough to guarantee the perfect life. The truth is probably the opposite: that our success is not about how big we can dream or how wonderful a life we feel we deserve, but how much discomfort and hard work we are willing to endure to get there.

Self-discipline is what keeps you going during those parts of the journey that just plain suck. If you decide that you will only remain engaged in something so long as it's interesting and pleasurable and easy to do so, you will always check out long before you have the chance to build something truly worthwhile and impressive. You'll simply flit from one shiny thing to the next, never achieving any real mastery, never developing yourself, never strengthening that muscle called your conscious intention.

You need the ability to deliberately decide that you will persist through difficulty, because the long-term goal is bigger and more important than your short-term discomfort and laziness. Can you see past this uncomfortable moment to the prize at the end?

Again, the trick is not that some people are capable of hard work and others aren't. Rather, it's that some people have convinced themselves that they *shouldn't* have to work hard, while others have accepted that it's an unavoidable part of the process, and just get on with it. Combine the belief that success should come easily with any of the blocks we've already discovered and you have a recipe for the so-called unexamined life, where all your dreams remain unfulfilled and you never know what you're really capable of.

Someone sees a friend building his own successful business, and says, "Wow, look at him go! I wish I had his energy. Must be nice." This is nothing but self-delusion, a fixed mindset and an inability to tolerate the discomfort he sees his successful friend dealing with. Underneath it all, this is a story that unconsciously says, "You are not meant to grow or be better. Success is not for you. Just stay small and unremarkable and never try anything."

Anytime we resist developing our own self-discipline, we are turning away from the only method that will bridge the gap between where we are now and where we want to be. There is no cheat code, no shortcut, no special way through. There is only hard work, and the courage and grit to decide that you will persevere even if it's unpleasant at times.

The saying goes, "The successful person has failed more times than the unsuccessful person has even tried." Think about it: the only difference between you and the successful person may be their higher tolerance for discomfort. There is a person out there, right now, with *less* inborn talent, privilege and luck than you, but who has nevertheless achieved more, simply because they were willing to fight harder for it.

Desiring instant gratification is a massive block to consciously designing the life you want. We need to be resilient and not flinch away from difficulty and hard work.

Discipline simply means: *Yes, laziness and fear, I acknowledge you, but I refuse to let you control me. No matter what, I'm going to act with integrity and pursue what's important.*

Nobody can make that decision but you. The good news is, the more you make that decision, the stronger your will becomes and the easier it is to make that choice the next time fear, laziness or temptation comes knocking.

The Curse of Inappropriate Expectations

Some say, "expectation is disappointment waiting to happen." There may be some truth in this, pessimistic as it sounds. Clinging to certain expectations is another way of saying that we hold unexamined beliefs about the world and ourselves. It's not wrong to hold these beliefs and expectations, but it can be difficult when our expectations are not met and our beliefs not confirmed.

Imagine you've gotten the idea to take up violin—you've always loved violin! You've seen countless live performances as well as recordings of "talented" people making gorgeous music. You've even seen young children playing beautifully, and heard of people learning to play well within just a few years. You're decided. You're going to play, too.

Perhaps unconsciously, you've already got some expectations of what it will be like to play the violin. So far, you've only seen people at recitals and performances, but never actually heard anyone practice. You've never heard what a beginner actually sounds like, or even what a bad player sounds like. Your head is so full of the beautiful music and the polished performances that when you finally pick up a violin yourself and drag the bow across the strings, you're horrified at how awful it sounds.

It *seemed* so much easier. Two weeks go by and your teacher can't even get you to make a single pleasing note. You had no idea how much effort and skill it takes simply to get the violin to *not* sound like a cat being strangled! So, what happens? You get impatient. Your teacher tells you it's normal and this is how everyone starts, even those virtuoso toddlers you've seen on YouTube.

But your expectations are badly off the mark. Focusing on the lovely end result, you've misunderstood what playing the violin is all about: hard work. A lot of it. Suddenly, the whole project isn't fun anymore. You were drawn to the instrument because of the beautiful music, because of how impressive it would be to play in front of others. When you decided to play violin, it was this vision you committed to—you never really agreed to the boring, frustrating and even embarrassing parts that actually take up most of a beginner violinist's journey.

Inappropriate expectations can lead us to be impatient, and to quit too early. We may expect ourselves to achieve more, and sooner, than is realistic. These expectations can also make us too hard on ourselves, so that we conclude we're a hopeless case and give up. With this mindset, you're not open to the *process* in front of you, which means you're not receptive to learning. Because you're so sure about how you think things *should* go, you're unable to adapt and move with changes in the situation as it actually *is*.

The person who understands from the outset that any achievement requires some sacrifice, hard work and effort is more likely to behave with resilience and a commitment to creative problem solving. *When you identify a new goal, are you committing to the fun end result, or all the work it takes to get there?* Many people get married, start a family, begin a degree or start a new job filled with expectations of all the benefits. But what happens when they're confronted with the bad sides? They're unprepared.

Having realistic expectations helps you to be patient, moderates your disappointment, and most importantly, encourages you to put in the hard work required. Nothing worthwhile is accomplished easily, or quickly. Understand this and you are leagues ahead of people who embark on projects based on whims and fantasies, only to quit the moment the illusion crumbles.

The Right Way and the Easy Way are Seldom the Same Way

A good way to get around the human tendency for "laziness," impatience and a low tolerance for discomfort is to grasp the way that *time* features in the process of achieving goals. It's a matter of perspective. When you are focused only on the present moment, your perception is concerned only with pleasures and pains right in front of you. But when you expand your awareness to include more long-term thinking, you give yourself the chance to think beyond what is happening in this moment right now.

Better yet, you can connect what is happening in the present moment to the bigger picture. If you've never really thought beyond today, you'll see any discomfort in the present as something to avoid and fix as soon as possible. But if you're able to contextualize your experience as part of a process that unfolds into the future, you are better able to see discomfort differently.

Rather than seeing pain and hardship as an impediment to what you want, you actually start to see it as *the means through which you achieve what you want.* "The obstacle is the path," as the old proverb goes. Unless you have a broad enough view, you can never look at difficulty and discomfort this way—it will always just seem like something unpleasant and unwanted. But if you know the purpose that discomfort serves, if you understand how this step fits into the plan at large, you uncover the strength to persist with it, rather than giving up.

Short-term thinking is short-sighted. You may decide to drop out of your university course prematurely because you're finding it too difficult. From a short-term perspective, this makes sense. By doing so you relieve tension and feel better, right now. But what is hidden from you in that moment is everything that you've lost *in the future* by choosing to quit.

You need to consider whether the temporary relief in the present moment of not having any study challenges is really bigger and better than the benefits gained from earning your degree. This is a tally that can be hard to make in real life. It's a normal human bias to give more weight to things going on in the present—after all, it's here where we literally feel and experience the situation. Compared to that, the future seems abstract and less important somehow. Less real.

Of course, you will have to face the consequences of every action you take today, in the future. Whether you acknowledge these consequences and take action to control them or not is entirely up to you, however. Many people meet life in the present only, living reactively, never truly claiming their power to determine how their future unfolds.

But that approach is the opposite of what we're trying to cultivate in this book. Being consciously aware of your full scope for conscious action also includes flexing your own agency in the future, not just right now. Acting in the moment is easy and impulsive. Acting in the moment *to achieve some specific aim in the future* takes more work—we need to envision our goal, even though it doesn't exist yet. We need to practice discipline to reach it, step by step, despite temptations and distractions in the moment.

Here's a good way to get better at long-term, conscious and deliberate thinking: remind yourself that the easy path only seems like what you want. In the longer term, it's usually the easy path that is *least* satisfying, impressive or lasting. We don't often think of it in this way, but the tradeoff is always between the small win now and the big win later. Is a life of endless little moments of self-indulgence really worth more than one of achievement, growth and satisfaction?

In the moment, the small temptation always seems more attractive, and the long-term reward always seems flimsy, far-off and uninspiring. But the trick to delayed gratification is realizing that this is an illusion—the easy path is often the path we don't really want, if only we look closely and are honest with ourselves.

There isn't a single famous person in history, no great scientist, prolific artist, esteemed philanthropist or genius philosopher, who got that way by choosing the easy path over the hard one. In fact, how many admired historical figures achieve fame and respect *because* of their ability to endure hardship, to stick to their vision even during the tough times, and to perform the challenging and groundbreaking feats that their peers were incapable of?

What is difficult and challenging is so often precisely what is optimal. Sow today what you want to reap tomorrow. Be satisfied with small, humble steps today because you know that in time, they add up to something truly wonderful.

Let's wrap up our chapter by returning to our four-step process, with a brief example.

Uncover: You may discover that you have this mental block of so-called "laziness" when you become aware of yourself procrastinating, engaging in distracting or addictive behaviors, or acting in ways that undermine the goals or values you claim to have for yourself. Maybe you notice that you start things frequently but seldom finish them, or that you flit around from plan to plan, never settling into the long haul with anything.

Perhaps you identify an unwillingness to tolerate discomfort in the fact that you cannot seem to quit smoking. You always seem to get mad cravings, and then cave in, deciding that you don't have the patience and can't be bothered. Behind this is a belief: *I must always act to avoid discomfort.*

Remove: By gently challenging this belief when it crops up, you can gradually start to replace it with a healthier one: *I am willing to endure discomfort to achieve what's important to me.*

Whether it's with nicotine cravings or any other temptation in life, you can start questioning the belief that change should be easy or simple. You can also regularly remind yourself that short-term indulgence is no longer going to be enough for you. You stop looking for magic tricks or quick cures. You adjust your expectations: to quit smoking, sooner or later you're going to have to go *through* your discomfort.

Reduce: Being unwilling to tolerate discomfort is not always a bad thing. In fact, with more conscious attention, you may become aware of something interesting: that you have been ignoring discomfort all along—the discomfort of being out of breath and having a horrible smoker's cough!

Tolerating what's bad for us doesn't make sense. Learning to put up with the discomfort of living a life we know is wrong for us is not a virtue. Ironically, learning to tolerate the discomfort we consciously choose can also leave us feeling more empowered to say no to discomfort that doesn't serve us.

Transform: How on earth could you transform a smoking habit into something useful?! The great thing about any bad habit is that it's still a habit—one that you can leverage for good. Every time you have the urge for a cigarette, use it as an invitation to practice a moment of mindfulness, take a few deep breaths, stretch, smile or read an affirmation. Piggyback good habits on bad ones while you work to get rid of them. At the very least, you are practicing your ability to remain conscious of just what you're doing, moment by moment. Through this step, you can turn an unwillingness to tolerate discomfort into a willingness to only tolerate the right problems, failures, and so on. You're still intolerant, but now it's toward the more appropriate issue.

Aside from examining your habits and beliefs, let's look externally for a moment.

Optimizing your environment for self-discipline really comes down to understanding how automatic most of your decision-making is.

To illustrate that point, consider the findings of a study conducted in eleven European countries on organ donors. The data showed that countries that automatically have citizens opted in to be organ donors—requiring action to opt out—had rates at or above 95 percent participation. When the default choice was not to be an organ donor, however, the highest rate found in any of the eleven countries was a mere 27 percent participation. Ultimately, people just went with the option that required the least effort. Their decision said nothing about their actual intention or desire to be an organ donor.

This same concept of defaulting to the more desirable choice can be applied to your own self-discipline. We're predisposed toward the choice that requires less effort and will happily accept whatever is in front of our faces. Being aware of human nature, you can make it easy for yourself to choose whichever options most benefit you while also making it as difficult as possible to make harmful decisions.

A default option is one that the decision-maker chooses if he or she does nothing, or makes the minimal amount of effort. In other contexts, default options also include those that are normative or suggested. Countless experiments and observational studies have shown that making an option the default will increase the likelihood of it being chosen, which is known as the default effect. Making decisions requires energy, so we often choose the default option to conserve energy, especially when we aren't familiar with what it is we are making a decision about.

Optimizing these default decisions is where the bulk of your efforts to create a more discipline-conducive environment can take place. You might believe that you control the majority of your choices, but in reality, that isn't the case. Instead, a significant amount of your actions are just responses to your environment.

If you're distracted by social media, for example, you might move the app icons to the back page of your phone so that you aren't constantly seeing them whenever you open your phone to do something else. Better yet, you can log out of the apps after each use or delete them from your phone altogether so that you'll only use them when you really want to, instead of letting them become distractions.

And if you're in the habit of mindlessly picking up your phone while working, you can simply start placing it facedown and far enough away that you have to get up to reach it. If you want to practice violin more, put the instrument on your desk with your music notes open. If you want to floss your teeth more often, keep floss in your backpack, in your bathroom, on your nightstand, and on your sofa.

There are seemingly endless examples of how you can utilize the default effect to become more disciplined with very little use of willpower itself. Another one is that leaving potato chips and cookies out on the kitchen counter will make it your default choice to eat those items whenever you walk through the kitchen feeling even the slightest bit hungry. Hiding those treats (or not buying them at all) and setting fruit out instead will instantly increase the probability that you eat fruit and that you avoid the unhealthy snacks. Want to exercise more? Put a pull-up bar in your bathroom doorway.

If you keep sugary sodas and juices in your refrigerator, you're making it your default choice to drink them whenever you are thirsty and open the fridge. But if you don't have those options, you increase the likelihood that you'll drink water, or make tea. Want to take more vitamins? Put them right next to your toothbrush for easier access.

If you sit in an office all day and have back problems, then you might benefit from standing up and walking frequently throughout the day. You can make this your default option by drinking water constantly so that you are forced to get up to go to the bathroom. Or perhaps you could schedule alarms on your phone and place it somewhere out of reach so that you have to stand up to turn off the alarm whenever it goes off.

The whole point of these examples is that you can save your willpower and your energy by making positive changes to your environment. The two biggest facets of environmental change are reducing clutter and distractions and optimizing choices based on the default effect.

If you reduce distractions from your environment, you'll clear your mind, which in turn increases focus, efficiency, and productivity. Furthermore, you can use your dopamine reward system to your advantage by reinforcing your own good habits with positive rewards, while also cutting back on mindless pursuits of small pleasures. Finally, you can make it so the path with the least effort leads to the choices you desire and benefit from.

These tactics all help you avoid actually using—and depleting—discipline so you can save it for your bigger daily challenges. After all, why exercise willpower when you don't need to if you can plan around it?

The takeaway:

- "Laziness" often masks the mental block of being unable to tolerate discomfort, or the belief that success shouldn't be challenging, difficult or take too long. It's not that "lazy" people are incapable of handling the hardships one needs to cope with for success; they've simply convinced themselves that they shouldn't have to, and so they never try. This is just another form of a fixed mindset and self-delusion which says we just don't have what it takes to be successful because we're "lazy." With self-discipline and hard work, we achieve what we set out to.

- An intolerance for the inevitable hard work of self-improvement sometimes comes down to inappropriate expectations. We need to be honest and realistic in what we expect from life, so that we don't give up too easily or assume that we're not talented enough to achieve our dreams.
- The right way is seldom the easy way. When we understand that growth and evolution can be difficult, we become more resilient and succeed sooner. We must also accept that the good life is never without its share of difficulties. The easy life is a myth, and no matter who you are, you'll need to make sacrifices before you can see the results you desire. These sacrifices are not an obstacle to what you want, but the way toward your goals.
- We can cultivate a success mindset by understanding that short-term gratification can never compare to the satisfaction of achieving our goals in the long-term. You can also apply

the uncover, remove, reduce, and transform rule to identify this fixed mindset, patiently replacing it with a willingness to tolerate discomfort, reducing the things we don't need to tolerate, and finally transforming the intolerance for discomfort into a tolerance for only the right discomforts.
- Aside from mindsets and retraining your beliefs, one way to have more self-discipline is to control and curate your environment. This is when we want to optimize our default decisions for self-discipline; in other words, make it easy to be good, and make it difficult to be bad. This is completely within your control.

Chapter 7: The Block of Close-Mindedness

Imagine someone who's experiencing serious and debilitating health concerns. The doctors are stumped. The person starts seeking alternative medicine options, but after lots of promising treatments, the condition persists. The person finally decides that their problems must be due to a food allergy, and if only they can stop eating the offending food, they'll get better.

They eliminate and re-introduce all the usual food culprits. The symptoms get worse. They eliminate *more* food groups—the resulting headaches and stomach troubles must be down to "detoxing," they think. The symptoms get worse. They're now more convinced than ever that their hard-to-pin-down food allergy was more dangerous than they thought. They end up telling everyone about this food allergy, rearrange their entire lives to accommodate a new diet, and even start educating others about the condition. Their symptoms get worse.

Many years later, a conventional doctor accidentally identifies the *real* problem: it has nothing to do with food at all, and is fixed within a matter of weeks with a commonly available medication. Oops.

It's easy to see what went wrong in this example—the person simply became too invested in one particular perspective. Unable to consider other alternatives, they got stuck seeing their situation in a narrow, fixed way, unable to absorb new information, adapt, question assumptions or drop old strategies when they simply didn't work anymore. Like a horse wearing blinkers, they have "tunnel vision" that actually prevents them from behaving in their own best interests.

This isn't to pick on alternative medicine, either—the story could have easily gone the other way, and most of us know of conventional doctors who doggedly pursue what they think is the problem, all the while missing the answer staring them in the face.

Nothing stops us from learning more than the belief that we already know what we need to know.

As human beings, we all need to make models of the world we find ourselves in. We need to make predictions, assumptions and best guesses—we would get nowhere if we didn't! The trick, however, is to know when to abandon an old model when presented with new information. An inaccurate perspective is only a problem if we fail to adjust it when we know better.

There are other limitations to being close-minded, a big one being how it makes you a real bore! Thinking you know it all already means you can't act with humility or curiosity. Every situation you encounter simply gets turned into extra proof of your particular viewpoint, whether it fits or not. You end up discounting other equally valid perspectives—including those that could have taught you something.

Getting overly attached to just one favorite viewpoint is actually the fastest way to ensure you learn nothing. Doing so makes you *feel* as if you know a lot, but in reality you're lacking self-awareness. What's more, how could you ever identify that you are mistaken if you're not even able to acknowledge the possibility?

Another obvious downside is that thinking you know everything makes you naturally more judgmental and intolerant of others. If you're correct, that naturally means that everyone else isn't. You have put yourself in a position where all difference is bad, and everyone who disagrees with you is plainly an idiot—what else would they be by disagreeing with the obvious truth?

You become worse at communication, and less willing to communicate in the first place, since there's not much to be gained, except perhaps the joy of lecturing others. Your original impulse came from wanting to know, but the cruel irony is that it leads you to shutting yourself off entirely from genuine knowledge.

As we saw in the fixed mindset chapter, not only are you less likely to be compassionate and understanding of others, but some of this judgmental attitude will reflect back on you, and you may be so self-critical that you never dare risk trying something new and different, for fear of being wrong.

Again, when it comes to success or failure, achieving goals, and fulfilling our true potential, it's all about *mindset*. It almost doesn't matter what adversity we encounter, what data we're faced with, what random events befall us, or the skills and qualities we're blessed with—what matters is how we frame it all, and how that perspective influences the way we act.

Just as we saw in the chapter on self-delusion, however, it can be tricky to really know how you're thinking, what mental models you're using, or how limited your perspective is. This is because a really useful model of the world will seem invisible, and you'll look at it and sincerely believe you're looking at reality itself, and not a model of reality.

The ability to honestly appraise your thought processes and *think about your thinking* is what distinguishes truly conscious, intentional people. Einstein famously said that you cannot solve a problem with the same thinking that created that problem in the first place. In the same way, we never really make big changes if we only work within our self-imposed limits—we need to step outside of them, and look at the limits themselves.

In our example, the person was engaging in purpose-driven, intentional and self-directed problem solving. But it didn't matter because the *frame* inside which they were doing it was inaccurate. They allowed a set of faulty assumptions to go unchallenged, and missed the real insight of the situation in front of them.

Quick, here's a question for you: Right now, what is your dominant way of interpreting the information that comes your way (including this question)?

We all like to think that we are *neutral;* that we are objective data-processing machines in an objective universe, and we are simply taking in information and responding to it. But we don't acknowledge a powerful intermediate step in which we *interpret* what we perceive. This interpretation is total, constant, and may happen without you being in the least aware of it.

Julia Galef's famous TED talk outlined what she saw as two fundamentally different mindsets, or approaches to interpreting incoming data from the world. The first she called a "soldier" mindset. The soldier approaches new information with a handful of beliefs they've already decided on. The aim is to defend and protect those beliefs from new data, if necessary—as though conflicting data were an enemy that needed to be shot down.

This was broadly the approach taken in our example. There was one key piece of new information that the person was bombarded with: the fact that their symptoms continually worsened, despite dietary changes. Their response to this new data was to double down on the already-held belief, even twisting conflicting information until it looked like evidence for the current model.

We can see this mindset any time we encounter warring factions, be they literal tribes and nations, or simply feuding families or groups who have decided they are one another's enemies—believers vs. atheists, liberals vs. conservatives, rich vs. poor and so on.

This reminds us of the fixed mindset—i.e. we settle on an idea *before* taking on new information, and new information is filtered according to what we already "know." As an example, consider a person who holds the sexist belief, "Women are bad drivers." One day they encounter a brilliant woman driver. This data point is a threat; the person simply concludes "well, they're kind of a masculine sort of woman anyway, they're clearly an exception."

The other approach in Galef's theory is the "scout," the person who is motivated by a desire to understand, learn and gain insight into the truth. This mindset is more flexible, since it is fundamentally curious and receptive. It's asking a question of the surrounding environment, rather than marching in with a forceful statement. This aligns neatly with the growth mindset we've explored—new information is not seen as a threat, challenge or competition, but something new and interesting to explore.

This is the mindset that would have allowed the person in our first example to notice the obvious fact of them not getting better on their new diet. Instead of all the mental gymnastics needed to see this information and *still* cling to the chosen model, the person could become curious: if it's not a food allergy, then what else could it be? They might have carried on their search and found the true solution much sooner.

The presence of an excellent woman driver might alert someone with a "scout" mindset to think again about their own assumptions and conclusions. They might decide, "Maybe this idea I have about women isn't really true after all." More likely, they wouldn't have believed in such a stereotype in the first place.

There are probably more mindsets than these two, and subtle variations of each. You could approach the world and the new information it contains with more or less active agency, more or less curiosity, more or less ego. You could view the world like a scientist, like a gambler, like a prey animal who sees threat everywhere, like a child, like a parent, like a businessman, as though it's a game, as though it's a gift, or as though it's an epic TV series that you're half-heartedly watching unfold as a mere spectator.

Whatever your orientation to reality itself, it's decidedly *not* neutral. We all like to think of ourselves as somehow centered, with our opinions and values being the obvious norm, while everyone *else* has biases, beliefs, preconceptions and so on. But of course, we have them, too.

At the root of either mindset is not rational thought, but emotion. The soldier approach is driven by fear and mistrust of difference and novelty. This is a basic emotional temperament that craves stability and fears the unknown. This is the person who gravitates toward tradition. Testing one's beliefs is seen as weak.

The scout is motivated by curiosity—the world feels like a more friendly and interesting place to them, so they don't respond with defensiveness, but interest. This is the person who gravitates toward novelty and innovation. Testing one's beliefs is seen as a strength.

To find out which mindset you may lean toward, ask yourself how you view changing your mind. Do you think that you've "won" an argument if you haven't budged at all and convinced the other person you're right? Do you think that admitting you were wrong is embarrassing?

When you meet someone with a different opinion than you, do you ask questions and become curious, or do you silently gear up for mental battle, thinking of all the ways you could prove them wrong? How do you see engagement with foreign ideas and the people that hold them? Are conversations a chance to learn, to bond socially, or to prove your superiority?

Many people think that being argumentative makes them intellectually formidable—in reality, the opposite is true.

Imagine two people get into a heated political discussion. They both see the discussion as an opportunity to prove which "team" is right, and to boast their superior knowledge and get the other to surrender. It's a matter of protecting their mutual egos—their entire identity and self-worth rests on whether they're perceived as right, i.e. better.

Can you imagine anything less productive, and less likely to lead to learning, understanding and insight for either person?

The first thing to do is acknowledge that being neutral or objective is an illusion: we all have a subjective perspective we're inhabiting, conscious or unconscious. Our culture is set up to reward the soldier mindset, unfortunately. Whether it's in business, politics, academics or science, so many of us go through the motions of learning or asking questions, when in reality we are only seeking to confirm what we already believe to be true.

Though most of us would like to be the scout, we're probably guilty of being the soldier more often than not. After all, isn't it only our ego's desire to belong to the "right" team (i.e. the scout) that makes us believe we're already functioning that way? Maybe you read the above section and thought, "Well, yes, sounds like a good idea—all those other people who are soldiers should clearly be more like me, a natural scout."

Becoming aware of and detaching from our bias is not easy, but it is simple. First, **uncover** why you inhabit this mindset. In fact, just noticing and admitting that you have this mindset in the first place gets you halfway there. Wanting to defend ourselves often comes from an unconscious belief that disagreement is the same as attack, and that there can only be one right person, so it had better be you!

Where did you first learn that being wrong was a weakness or flaw? Where did you learn that the point of mastery and understanding was not for its own sake, but as a way to bolster the ego?

Try to detach your own identity and sense of worth from your beliefs. If you catch yourself in the soldier mindset, remind yourself that there is no "war," metaphorically speaking. Try some of the following affirmations to gently challenge and **remove** this mindset when you notice it crop up:

"It's OK for me and others to change our minds."
"My beliefs are provisional, and I am always open to learning more."
"I have value and worth as a human being, no matter whether I'm right or wrong."
"I learn for the joy of learning."
"I do not have to compete, convince, or prove anything to anyone."

Of course, sometimes your beliefs *are* worth holding on to. Sometimes, it's worthwhile to be able to defend and justify your position, not to prove your superiority to your opponent, but to clarify for *yourself* why you hold the ideas you do.

We can **reduce** the effect of this mental block by carefully considering our own perspectives as rationally and objectively as possible. If we have to see anything as a threat to defend against, it can't hurt to imagine our own ignorance, bias and irrationality as the real "enemy." Can we transform our soldier mindset into one where we are fully on guard for closed-mindedness in ourselves?

A great way to do this practically is to search out the opposite to our usual impulse—instead of finding reasons to support what we already think, can we actively seek out evidence to disprove it? Though this may feel uncomfortable at first, you'll ultimately be a better-informed person who will see the gray areas in everything that appeared black and white. Nobody likes discovering that they are wrong about something, but you can transform your closed-mindedness about foreign ideas to a perspective which refuses to consider that there is only one possible explanation for any phenomena. Through this mindset, you avoid the binary thought process where one party is either right or wrong. Instead, we all simply look at things differently in equally valid ways.

If all else fails, try to think like Charles Darwin, as he had a particular view on stepping outside of his own perspective. The very basic guideline of Darwin's golden rule was to be more than just open to contradicting or opposing ideas—indeed, Darwin gave them his fullest attention:

"I had, also, during many years, followed a golden rule, namely, that whenever a published fact, a new observation or thought came across me, which was opposed to my general results, to make a memorandum of it without fail and at once; for I had found by experience that such facts and thoughts were far more apt to escape from memory than favorable ones."

Darwin completely immersed himself in evidence or explanations that went against his findings because he was aware that the human mind is inclined to dispose of those contrary views. If he didn't investigate them as fully as he could, he'd be likely to forget them, and that would create mental dishonesty. Darwin knew that his own instinctual thinking could be a hindrance to finding the truth as much as it could help, and he established a way to ensure he wasn't missing out on any information.

Darwin handled all this conflicting information responsibly. He genuinely considered material that might have disproved his assertions and took pains to fully absorb every single scenario, anomaly, and exception to his theories. He didn't filter out information that didn't support his beliefs; he was utterly immune to confirmation bias. More than anything else, Darwin didn't want to be careless in finding the truth—he knew that a half-cocked assertion solely intended to persuade others without much thought was intellectually dishonest. Questioning his own beliefs required more time and effort on his part, but he was committed.

Uniquely, Darwin forces a dialogue of skepticism back to himself instead of to others in defensiveness. To himself, he would direct questions such as, "What do you know?" "Are you sure?" "Why are you sure?" "How can it be proved?" "What potential errors could you have made?" "Where is this conflicting view coming from and why?" Darwin accurately realized that if you hold the belief that everyone *else* is wrong, you're in trouble.

The takeaway:

- Closed-mindedness is failing to be aware of the mental perspective we inhabit—and so failing to see that we can and often should step outside of it. This traps us into thinking that we know everything, because what we've decided in our minds is the only possible outcome. When things don't turn out the way we expect, it makes us less compassionate toward ourselves and prevents personal growth.
- Our attitude toward new information determines the extent of our learning. If we are "soldiers" who seek only to defend the beliefs we already have, we don't grow or learn. But as "scouts" we learn for its own sake, reaching out in curiosity and receptivity. We aren't afraid of the truth; instead we actively seek to learn from it and improve ourselves.
- We all have a native perspective, a set of assumptions, a non-neutral attitude and even unconscious bias. Yet, we all believe that we are the unbiased ones who look at everything objectively and without

letting our emotions cloud our judgement. We only develop as people when we become conscious of these fallacies—and conscious of our ability to choose something different.
- Part of critical thinking is deliberately seeking out evidence against our chosen beliefs, rather than only seeking data that confirms them. Look for reputable sources and inform yourself about various things that are important to you. Inevitably, you'll discover that some of your beliefs were mistaken or simply naïve, but that is a surefire sign of growth as well.
- If all else fails, abide by Darwin's Golden Rule of trying to poke holes in your own argument. After all, it's better if you do it rather than someone else.

Summary Guide

CHAPTER 1: TURN OFF AUTOPILOT

- Intentional thinking is the conscious, willful control of your own thought processes so that you can actively direct your own life toward success. By thinking intentionally, you determine your own place in the world and gain control of your daily life.
- Thoughts have power, and our attitude and mindset create our world. The worst tragedies can be overcome if you have the right approach and use intentional thinking to respond to challenges in the most growth-oriented manner possible.
- Passivity, apathy, reactivity, failing to take responsibility, and failing to own our agency means we never achieve our goals, or even identify them in the first place. We are at the mercy of

fleeting whims, fears, or the wishes of others, and cannot follow our own true path or purpose.
- Mental blocks can impede our ability to think intentionally. Examples are self-deception, closed-mindedness, fear of discomfort, indecisiveness and self-doubt. Given how essential our thoughts are to who we are, what we do, how we perceive the world around us and exist in it, and so on, these mental blocks need to be carefully replaced with healthier modes of thinking.
- Throughout this book, we'll use the formula "uncover, remove, reduce, and transform" to address these mental blocks and develop intentional thinking. We can tackle mental blocks by uncovering their cause, removing them by challenging our self-talk, beliefs and assumptions, reducing the impact these blocks have on our lives, and slowly transforming this part of ourselves into something beneficial.

CHAPTER 2: THE BLOCK OF SELF-DOUBT

- The mental block of self-doubt can show up in the form of imposter syndrome, where we choose to listen to our negative self-belief rather than the objective evidence of our success. We could be the best at what we do, yet some of us suffer from a nagging suspicion that our successes are a result of pure chance, and that fate, not merit, has made us successful. As such, you might fear being discovered for the incompetent self you really are.
- The narrative of a person suffering from imposter syndrome is just one of many that we could tell ourselves. Our core self-beliefs inform the stories we tell about ourselves—and these narratives often work against us.
- We can change our core beliefs by slowly reworking our self-narratives. We can do this by accepting our negative emotions with self-compassion and curiosity, before we gently rewrite our stories. Avoid the temptation to compare yourself to others, especially if you are active on social media. Places like Instagram

make you feel bad about your life because you're constantly subjected to a barrage of updates with all of your friends posting about their successes, vacations, etc. However, it is important to remember that nobody posts their failures and dull moments, and that their reality is likely to be much closer to your own.
- When we slow down and become curious about why we feel as we do, we can start to reduce, remove and transform negative self-belief into a feeling of self-love and high self-esteem. Other practical ways to reinforce a confident mindset are to dress the part and spend time grooming yourself the way someone who values themselves would, and cultivate the right mental biases which look for the silver lining in every negative outcome.

CHAPTER 3: THE BLOCK OF INDECISION

- Indecisiveness comes down to an intolerance of uncertainty, and often to informational overload. In our modern, technologically advanced world, we're constantly bombarded with an endless set of options in all spheres of life. We're also saturated with all the information we come across on a daily basis, and this makes it hard to decide on things because we're always looking for a better choice. We can consciously decide, however, to embrace imperfection and take on risks in the service of achieving what we care about.

- Another way to tackle information overload is to ascertain what you need to know in order to make a decision, and identify the outcome you're looking for. Then, narrow down possible decisions and take a leap of faith by choosing any because the opportunity cost involved becomes very low.
- Our fear of the unknown is something we have inherited from our ancestors because for most of human history, being suspicious of what we didn't know kept us alive and free from dangers. However, in the modern world, this fear can

become catastrophic because we are constantly asked to make choices in areas where we have incomplete knowledge. In today's world, acting without knowing all the details is often necessary to avoid becoming paralyzed, and is unlikely to lead to the extreme danger it did in the distant past.
- We can become more decisive by applying the four steps of uncover, remove, reduce and transform. Critical thinking and data gathering are useful—if our target is healthy, and if it ultimately serves the end goal of conscious *action*. However, at some point we need to commit to taking an action. Think about whether a particular decision will take you closer to where you want to be, and if it does, go ahead with it.

We can make better decisions when we slow down, turn inward to appraise our own values, and simplify our choices. We can also remember that it's OK to make mistakes—that's how we learn.

CHAPTER 4: THE BLOCK OF FIXED MINDSET

- A fixed mindset is one where you believe that all of your qualities such as intelligence, motivation levels, your skills, and so on, are all inherently a part of you in pre-decided quantities that cannot ever be changed. This mindset precludes growth and the cultivation of our conscious intention; it tells us that any effort to improve is ultimately meaningless, because you can never be better than you already are.
- Instead, we can adopt a growth mindset and engage our conscious will to choose the self and the life we want, rather than passively accept the status quo. We tell ourselves that with the right amount of effort and the correct approach, we can be the person we want to be. If we aren't good at something, enough practice will help us improve and eventually master that activity.
- With a growth mindset, we see failure as the gift it is: an opportunity to learn and prove that we are evolving and changing. Fixed mindsets teach us that failures are

something to be scared of, and to avoid because they are a damning indictment of us as individuals. We view them as judgments rather than as merely part of the process of learning. However, growth mindsets help us see failures in a positive light because they represent the potential to be better.

- We can develop a growth mindset by abandoning grand goals somewhere off in the distance and instead focus on tiny, consistent daily habits that bring us closer and closer to excellence. Having a growth mindset involves valuing the process over the outcome, letting go of outlandish expectations for ourselves, accepting our shortcomings, and prioritizing learning to improve above all else.

CHAPTER 5: THE BLOCK OF SELF-DECEPTION

- Self-delusion is the biggest mental block to our full and honest awareness. All of us delude ourselves about reality to some extent; it is nothing to be ashamed of. However, self-deception has many negative consequences for our growth as individuals, and we must identify what it is about our lives that we have chosen to blind ourselves to, in order to avoid ignoring opportunities to work on our flaws.

- We know self-delusion is at play if we recognize defense mechanisms, which develop to protect our ego from uncomfortable truths. Nobody can tackle our defense mechanisms but us. There are many common mechanisms such as denial, repression, regression, projection, displacement, etc. Each can be identified through its own unique indicators, but the thing unifying them all is that they allow us to stay in a comfortable bubble where we can get away with not challenging ourselves enough to experience substantial growth.
- To live with more integrity and honesty, we need to acknowledge that growth and comfort are mutually exclusive. Can we accept *all* that we are, even the dark and

unwanted parts of ourselves? We must, because that is the only way we can ever improve. Pain, failure, mistakes; all of these are a part of life and we must not run away from them, because life is a package deal. The good life is never lived in a state of comfort devoid of hardships.
- When we can embrace our vulnerabilities with honesty and self-compassion, we can empower ourselves to act with more focused intention—and live the life we want.

CHAPTER 6: THE BLOCK OF DISCOMFORT

- "Laziness" often masks the mental block of being unable to tolerate discomfort, or the belief that success shouldn't be challenging, difficult or take too long. It's not that "lazy" people are incapable of handling the hardships one needs to cope with for success; they've simply convinced themselves that they shouldn't have to, and so they never try. This is just another form of a fixed mindset and

self-delusion which says we just don't have what it takes to be successful because we're "lazy." With self-discipline and hard work, we achieve what we set out to.
- An intolerance for the inevitable hard work of self-improvement sometimes comes down to inappropriate expectations. We need to be honest and realistic in what we expect from life, so that we don't give up too easily or assume that we're not talented enough to achieve our dreams.
- The right way is seldom the easy way. When we understand that growth and evolution can be difficult, we become more resilient and succeed sooner. We must also accept that the good life is never without its share of difficulties. The easy life is a myth, and no matter who you are, you'll need to make sacrifices before you can see the results you desire. These sacrifices are not an obstacle to what you want, but the way toward your goals.
- We can cultivate a success mindset by understanding that short-term

gratification can never compare to the satisfaction of achieving our goals in the long-term. You can also apply the uncover, remove, reduce, and transform rule to identify this fixed mindset, patiently replacing it with a willingness to tolerate discomfort, reducing the things we don't need to tolerate, and finally transforming the intolerance for discomfort into a tolerance for only the right discomforts.

- Aside from mindsets and retraining your beliefs, one way to have more self-discipline is to control and curate your environment. This is when we want to optimize our default decisions for self-discipline; in other words, make it easy to be good, and make it difficult to be bad. This is completely within your control.

CHAPTER 7: THE BLOCK OF CLOSE-MINDEDNESS

- Closed-mindedness is failing to be aware of the mental perspective we inhabit—and so failing to see that we

can and often should step outside of it. This traps us into thinking that we know everything, because what we've decided in our minds is the only possible outcome. When things don't turn out the way we expect, it makes us less compassionate toward ourselves and prevents personal growth.
- Our attitude toward new information determines the extent of our learning. If we are "soldiers" who seek only to defend the beliefs we already have, we don't grow or learn. But as "scouts" we learn for its own sake, reaching out in curiosity and receptivity. We aren't afraid of the truth; instead we actively seek to learn from it and improve ourselves.
- We all have a native perspective, a set of assumptions, a non-neutral attitude and even unconscious bias. Yet, we all believe that we are the unbiased ones who look at everything objectively and without letting our emotions cloud our judgement. We only develop as people when we become conscious of

these fallacies—and conscious of our ability to choose something different.
- Part of critical thinking is deliberately seeking out evidence against our chosen beliefs, rather than only seeking data that confirms them. Look for reputable sources and inform yourself about various things that are important to you. Inevitably, you'll discover that some of your beliefs were mistaken or simply naïve, but that is a surefire sign of growth as well.
- If all else fails, abide by Darwin's Golden Rule of trying to poke holes in your own argument. After all, it's better if you do it rather than someone else.

www.ingramcontent.com/pod-product-compliance
Lightning Source LLC
Chambersburg PA
CBHW071344080526
44587CB00017B/2951